A Virtual Care Blueprint

A Virtual Care Blueprint

How Digital Health Technologies Can Improve Health Outcomes, Patient Experience, and Cost-effectiveness

Robert L. Longyear III
Foreword by Dr. Greg Weidner, MD, FACP

Routledge
Taylor & Francis Group
A PRODUCTIVITY PRESS BOOK

First published 2022
by Routledge
600 Broken Sound Parkway #300, Boca Raton FL, 33487

and by Routledge
2 Park Square, Milton Park, Abingdon, Oxon, OX14 4RN

Routledge is an imprint of the Taylor & Francis Group, an Informa business

ISBN: 978-1-032-04409-5 (hbk)
ISBN: 978-0-367-65094-0 (pbk)
ISBN: 978-1-003-19306-7 (ebk)

Typeset in Minion
by Apex CoVantage, LLC

For my mom, relentlessly pursuing better

Contents

Foreword

A Virtual Care Blueprint by Robert L. Longyear III

> Change is the law of life, and those who look only to the past or present are certain to miss the future.
>
> **—John F. Kennedy**

What makes a moment? Merriam-Webster defines the word *moment* in a variety of ways, among them "a stage in historical or logical development," "importance in influence or effect," "a time of excellence or conspicuousness," and (as in physics) a "tendency or measure of tendency to produce motion especially about a point or axis." Few would dispute that in the realm of healthcare, by any or all of these definitions, this is a *moment*. Historic, important, conspicuous, and spinning the world of healthcare on its axis. We don't yet know how history will remember the moment that is 2020 (and the years that follow) as healthcare responds to, recovers from, and reimagines itself in the wake of the Covid-19 pandemic. How will it influence the industry and deliver excellence to those we serve? What lasting motion will it produce? Around which axis? In the pages that follow, Robert Longyear III addresses these and other important questions.

As I have worked in healthcare transformation for several decades, many have heard me speak about the "perfect storm moment"—joining a chorus of other leaders working in this space who collectively shared a vision for healthcare's future. Some of the many components of the perfect storm included shifting consumer expectations; the emergence and adoption of smartphones and wearables; evolving healthcare payment models; an epidemic of noncommunicable chronic disease; unsustainable cost curves; and advances in telehealth, connectivity, communication channels, remote diagnostics, and applied data/analytics capabilities. Over the last ten years, it was reasonable to imagine a world of empowered patients, connected to skilled, empathetic care teams via technology. Technology and data would also provide the power to scale and efficiently deliver personalized, high-value health and care by leveraging care models and experience design and skill-optimized teams.

I have had the opportunity to help create this vision and translate it into reality within a large healthcare system—building a primary care model based on digital-forward, whole-person, team-based care optimized for value. Our team had the unique opportunity to catalyze the conversion of this potential energy into kinetic energy and to see firsthand the impact it had on human lives, health engagement, experience of care, and measurable clinical outcomes. Thus inspired, none of us—care team or patients— would choose to go back to traditional models of care delivery even as we work toward advancing the vision in new and different ways. As I started writing this foreword, I dug back through presentations and found my first "perfect storm" reference nearly a decade ago. While we have seen real but incremental progress toward this vision, it's fair to say that real transformation across the industry has largely been in its early stages.

Then, in 2020, the Covid-19 pandemic seeded the perfect storm's clouds with silver iodide and made it rain in real and tangible ways for all involved in healthcare. Cycles of change and adoption usually measured in years or decades suddenly occurred in days and weeks. Necessity drove innovation and execution across the healthcare landscape and removed barriers for both providers and patients/ consumers. Government and commercial payors, regulators, and technology companies acted swiftly to remove friction and allow necessary care to proceed in this moment of crisis. Telehealth suddenly became *the* way to deliver care, without qualification by use case, geography, or other limitations. Reimbursement and regulatory pivots enabled this emergency deployment to proceed. Provider organizations adjusted their operations quickly and purposefully to address patient needs. Frontline healthcare heroes adapted, and their patients responded and engaged. The perfect storm, building in the skies for a decade, drenched the landscape and became an actual moment.

Given this forced convergence of multiple emerging trends, it's easy to believe that history will mark this moment as one that was the *beginning* of the digital health era even though much of its foundation had been built over more than two decades. The next phase of healthcare transformation and digital health will be defined in the coming years, as leaders execute on strategies to meaningfully connect the dots of these converging trends and deliver personalized, convenient, value-based, technology-enabled "quadruple aim" care. We will address chronic dis-ease, and the behaviors that impact them, within the fabric of patients' lives on a daily basis rather than in an exam room for 15 minutes each quarter. We will help people understand and navigate the complexity of healthcare so that it becomes more comprehensible and manageable. We will leverage skill-optimized, high-performing teams armed with facile technologies and predictive data streams. Healthcare technology will be deployed to extend and enhance the relationship that people have with their health and their healthcare team and to streamline and automate the transactional drag that often threatens these relationships. We will expand our definition of health beyond the mere absence of disease or infirmity and address the personal, emotional, social, and environmental determinants of health. There is work to be done, to be sure, on all these components—and this is the moment that will motivate and catalyze these changes in our industry.

Enter Robert Longyear III, the author of *Innovating for Wellness: Bridging the Gap Between Health System and Patient.* In this, his second book, Robert builds on the foundation of that excellent work with a deep dive into digital health and its critical role in the redesign of healthcare. From the first time I met Robert, in 2019, it was obvious that this was a young man with impressive intellect, education, experience, and pas-sion for deeply understanding healthcare as it is—with the deliberate and ambitious intent to use that understanding as a foundation for building the new healthcare *as it should be.* Driven by both personal and profes-sional experiences, Robert continues to build a network of change-makers and a voice which resonates with the song of healthcare transformation. In *A Virtual Care Blueprint,* Robert uses interviews, research and evidence, narratives, and aspirational visions of a digitally enabled experience to help us all better imagine this new healthcare. He provides valuable insights on telemedicine, remote-patient monitoring, patient engagement, chronic disease management, digital therapeutics, data collection, and payment policy to promote understanding, strategic, and tactical implementation of digitally enabled models of care.

In *A Virtual Care Blueprint,* Robert challenges all of us to embrace this vision as a professional and moral imperative and to dedicate our exper-tise, creativity, energy, and collaborative spirit to transform healthcare. As one who shares the vision, I stand firmly with him in this call to action and in working to inspire others to see it, believe it, and pursue it. In this moment, are you ready to make it happen?

Greg
Gregory R. Weidner, MD, FACP, DipABLM

Preface

My editor sent me a note requesting a few outstanding items after I submitted my first draft manuscript for this book. One of those items was this preface. A preface is not necessarily required for a book, but I could not refrain from the opportunity to add some pithy commentary on the writing process, digital health, and the Covid-19 pandemic. That is, after all, the point of a preface, isn't it? It also represents an opportunity to use the word "pithy," for which it is surprisingly hard to find a place in the main text of a book like this one.

To start off, let's take a brief foray into how this all started. I originally reached out to Routledge, Taylor & Francis, to see whether an editor would publish my first book, *Innovating for Wellness*. Shortly after finishing and publishing said book, Kristine Mednansky, the future editor for this book, called me and said she was interested. I told her she was about two days too late, but when a publisher like Routledge, Taylor & Francis, says they want to publish your book—you take it seriously. We came to the conclusion that it was too late to publish my first book because it had gone live on Amazon two days prior, and so after about 25 minutes of conversation, we agreed that I would write another book.

This decision was reached in April 2020, while I was standing in Meridian Hill Park in Washington, D.C., during the first wave of the Covid-19 pandemic. It was an uncertain time, as I had just started a new job launching a virtual care company incubated out of a three-year-old digital clinical staffing marketplace company. Did I feel ready to write an entirely new book? No. But this was a big moment in time for whatever you want to call it, telemedicine, virtual care, health tech, or the digital health industry. Covid-19 changed the game, as healthcare regulators and payors made important changes needed to support a struggling health system as in-person services became too dangerous due to infection risk. These changes and payment adjustments led to an explosion of interest in and a pressing need for digital health technologies and virtual care models.

Before we go any further, I'd like to take a moment to offer you a word of caution. If you think that you will likely have excess time on your hands to take on the task of writing a book during a raging respiratory virus pandemic due to the expectation that physical distancing and cancelled events would produce a time surplus—you'd be wrong. Sure, I had *some* more time on my hands as the D.C. happy hour scene tanked quickly in early March and I maintained a cautious approach in the months after to mitigate the risk of infection. But, like many people, my attention span was limited as the events of 2020 were riveting, yet stressful, leading to mind- and energy-consuming days. On most days, it was just easier to get out of the house after work to go for a walk. Sitting on the same computer used for the hours of Zoom meetings during the workday working in digital health and attempting to write about digital health was a daily struggle. But, nonetheless, I persevered and while I missed my self-imposed deadline by two months, Kristine was kind enough to give me the space to finish. In my experience, books are never really finished, just completed and extended into the next one.

I wrote this book for two primary reasons—first, I felt as though I personally needed to focus in more depth on some of the topics covered in my first book. I am the first to admit that I covered a bit too much ground to go into sufficient detail on any one topic. I feel like my first book served its purpose as the proving ground for the process of writing a book. I assure you, future authors, that the second one comes much more naturally than the first. Organizationally, scientifically, and with a clear point of focus, this book is written for a healthcare-innovator audience rather than the more general audience of the first. It allowed me to satisfy a lingering need to dig much deeper into a few topics—specifically, remote-patient monitoring (RPM) and hybrid virtual care models.

Second, and more importantly, I want to equip healthcare decision-makers, innovators, and policymakers with important, evidence-based information about virtual care and RPM. Technology has quickly outpaced traditional healthcare services and the ability of leaders to keep up. The modalities stemming from these technologies will continue to grow in scope and scale. Rapidly, they will begin to displace traditional models of care. As with anything with strong commercial growth prospects, the healthcare innovation market often suffers from a "marketing material" blitz where the scientific evidence, useful program information, and patient perspective are replaced by buzzwords, sales tactics, and curated single-patient case studies. The digital health industry has the opportunity not just to disrupt the traditional, failed models of healthcare services but to leave healthier and happier patients in its wake.

While I cover a number of technology-augmented care models in this book, I want to paint a picture of the type of virtual care that will most likely deliver positive long-term results for patients, health systems, and societies. These are those that balance human elements with all the benefits of technology and that are carefully designed from the patient's perspective. High-touch, relationship-based, data-driven virtual care models are scalable and effective. In doing so, I encourage everyone to expand their lexicon and conversations from audio-visual telemedicine to more comprehensive, multimodal models of virtual care targeted at high-prevalence chronic conditions.

In this same vein, I have been asked countless times about learning resources on digital health, virtual care, or RPM, but there aren't many currently available as of 2021. Truthfully, actual and credible information on virtual care and RPM is surprisingly difficult to find outside of a few academic centers of excellence, private companies, and content marketing materials pulled from the Centers for Medicare and Medicaid Services (CMS) website. I hope this book acts as a much-needed resource for future innovators and healthcare leaders looking to transform care delivery.

My interest in this type of care model stems from my experience as a caregiver for my mom. In 2012, she was diagnosed with a rare form of leukemia called chronic myeloid leukemia (CML). I will never forget the exact moment when she told me. Eight years later, I received a call that I will equally never forget. I was standing in a clean laboratory environment in the middle of Georgetown's Lombardi Comprehensive Cancer Center wearing full personal protective equipment, when my dad called to inform me that my mom was in the emergency room with a condition called blast crisis—essentially, where her seven years of well-controlled, in-remission CML spiraled out of control as cancerous white blood cells quickly multiplied. In the months after, we traversed hospitalization, chemotherapy, outpatient care, home healthcare and, eventually, hospice care. In this, we experienced both the successes and failures of the modern chronic disease healthcare journey. I was 20 years old at the time and, as it should have, this experience set me on my current path.

It is becoming overwhelmingly clear to me that we have the tools and knowledge we need to transform the way healthcare is delivered in the United States and in countries around the world. Implementation and societal-level adoption are lagging behind. The academic and policy circles, both with significant influence on the ways in which healthcare is delivered, are still largely trying to figure out older models of telemedicine and have not even begun to catch up to the advances in technologies available to today's clinicians and healthcare organizations. RPM and more comprehensive models of virtual care are here and effective, but implementation is significantly hindered by the limited understanding of policymakers and the academic-medicine-industrial complex. The old mental models of healthcare held by the masses are being rapidly challenged by technology and new innovations in care delivery. The lines are becoming blurred quickly.

No matter who you are, we can all agree that, in its current form, healthcare is not working.

It's time to rethink how, where, from whom, and when healthcare is delivered.

I hope this book inspires, educates and, at the very least, leads to much-needed critical thinking. For humanity, for societies around the world, and for everyday patients—we have an imperative to pursue any means of producing better health.

Acknowledgments

Special thanks to:

Dr. Richard Boxer, MD
Dr. Greg Weidner, MD
Dr. Faisel Syed, MD
Angie Stevens, BSN, RN
Dr. Jerry Wilmink, PhD
Caroline Adams
Zia Rahman
Mark Silverman, JD

Your impact on healthcare is and will continue to be apparent. Thank you for your stories, your expertise, and your friendship.

Author

Robert L. Longyear III is VP of Digital Health and Innovation at Wanderly and its sister company, Avenue Health. His first book, *Innovating for Wellness*, explores the intersection of health policy and health technology innovation. Originally from Marietta, Georgia, Robert lives in Washington, D.C., where he enjoys the restaurant scene, policy events, and happy hour.

Robert has worked across the healthcare industry for a number of organizations including Medicaid Health Plans of America in policy analysis, WellCare Health Plans in clinical quality improvement, and the Institute for Medicaid Innovation (IMI). At the IMI, he led two research projects in conjunction with major Medicaid health plans looking at national best practices in high-risk care coordination and social determinants of health data collection. In his career in health technology, Robert was Director of Product at a pharmacy-focused mHealth technology company, where he took the company to a contract with the United States Air Force and lead the submission of three National Institutes of Health Small Business Innovation Research (SBIR) grant proposals. In biotechnology, Robert worked for Synergene Therapeutics, while in school, studying the pharmacokinetics of nanotechnology-delivered p53 gene therapy in solid tumors. Robert has consulted for several innovative biotechnology and digital health companies, from start-ups to market leaders.

His research work has been published by the IMI, *NEJM Catalyst*, and the American Psychological Association's *Practice Innovations* journal. His main focus is on innovations for healthcare delivery and care management as well as the application of digital health technologies to healthcare services, broadly. Specifically, Robert has expertise in remote patient monitoring, virtual care, and the use of digital experiences to solve problems in healthcare services.

Robert hosts live webinar series with Dr. Faisel Syed, Head of Primary Care at ChenMed, where they discuss key topics in healthcare innovation such as the full-risk primary care model, Medicare Advantage for all, virtual care, telemedicine, the social determinants of health, and care coordination for high-risk patients.

He graduated *cum laude* from Georgetown University with a degree in healthcare management and policy and went on to complete his thesis on innovative payment and care delivery system reform efforts in state Medicaid programs—specifically, innovative state adaptations of the Accountable Care Organization model stemming from the Medicare Shared Savings Program. At Georgetown, Robert also received his national certification as an emergency medical technician.

When Robert was 20, his mom's chronic myeloid leukemia spiraled out of control and he became a caregiver for a high-risk patient with multiple chronic conditions as she fought for her life. The six months spent navigating the healthcare system from outpatient care, to inpatient care and, eventually, to palliative care provided firsthand education on health system failures. This experience provides a dual view of healthcare from both the patient and system perspectives.

You can connect with Robert L. Longyear III on LinkedIn and @ RLLongyear on Twitter.

1

Introduction

I walked into the bathroom of Union Market in Washington, D.C., around mid-February 2020. With the recent reports of a SARS-like virus circulating in China, I was wary of going to a place with such a large number of people. I made my way into line at the bathroom and waited—as one does. Shortly after getting into line, I noticed an employee of Union Market enter and move toward the sinks to look in the mirror. He coughed a few times and looked visibly sick as he proceeded to wash his face in the sink.

I quickly left the bathroom, found some hand sanitizer, and motioned to my friend outside that we should leave to go somewhere less crowded and not indoors. A few days later, the first confirmed cases of the virus, now named Sars-CoV-2, began to appear in the United States and other countries around the world. It took a matter of weeks for the virus, and its disease Covid-19, to reach the level of a pandemic.

As a respiratory disease, Covid-19 spreads rapidly between persons. To combat the exponential spread, public health authorities across the globe recommended societal lockdowns, social distancing, and mask mandates. With the lockdowns came paradoxical effects for healthcare systems around the world and in the United States. Some service lines that provide elective or non-emergency care saw forced shutdowns, while others like intensive care units and emergency departments were flooded with patients experiencing a wide variety of cardiopulmonary symptoms and distress.

Given the infection risk, healthcare organizations, clinics, and medical offices represented unsafe locations, and thus healthcare visit volumes[1] decreased rapidly (~60% reduction) at the beginning of the pandemic in the United States and globally. In-person services became unsafe—thus the health system, at large, turned to modern technologies to maintain connection with patients.

It's been called a revolution, an unprecedented boost, a windfall, an accelerator, ten years of progress in a month, and Covid-19. For healthcare's slow move to digital, the pandemic accelerated adoption and exposure to what could be the future. Call it what you want—telehealth, telemedicine, virtual care, digital health—whatever it's called, the Covid-19 pandemic forced regulators and healthcare organizations to quickly mobilize technologies to continue providing needed care to patients as in-person services became unsafe.

To quote then Centers for Medicare and Medicaid Services Administrator Seema Verma, with regard to this topic, "I think the genie's out of the bottle on this one. I think it's fair to say that the advent of telehealth has been just completely accelerated, that it's taken this crisis to push us to a new frontier, but there's absolutely no going back."

Patients needed care and providers needed revenue to continue operating. Thus, in the midst of a pandemic, the immediate solution sat firmly in the provision of services remotely and via digital technologies—and that's exactly what happened.

The reports all tell the same story. Electronic medical record (EMR) company eClinicalWorks reported an increase from 100,000 minutes of televisits on March 16, 2020, to 1.5 million by April 6, 2020, through their Healow telehealth brand. Similarly, data[2] from Epic Systems, another large EMR vendor, was published by Fox et al.(2020) showing a 300-fold increase in telehealth visits. In mid-April, the first peak of the virus in the US, telehealth visits represented 69% of all visits among health systems using Epic according to the data published by Fox et al.

Telehealth had been on the rise in the US, and globally, since the early 2000s. But a number of barriers to adoption made the growth of this care delivery modality slow. In 2020, Covid-19 forced health systems, regulators, governments, physicians, and patients to adopt.

As I lived through this event while writing this book on the topic, I was fortunate to have a front row seat to the growth, the challenges, and the opportunities now presented in the world of telehealth. At the same time, the period was marked by tremendous uncertainty, fear, and enormous loss. While a windfall for the digital health industry, Covid-19 wreaked havoc on all facets of society and on the lives of individuals. Intensive care units (ICUs) were filled to the brim with patients in respiratory failure.

General Motors and other large companies began manufacturing ventilators. People lost their jobs. Hundreds of thousands lost their lives to a complex respiratory virus. And the population experienced incredible stress from fear of infection, grief, and an uncertain future.

In the midst of the early pandemic, I thought back to my life a few years prior. In March of 2017, my family was in the throes of the toughest year of our collective lives. My mom, a leukemia survivor of eight years, was hospitalized as her condition entered a state known as blast crisis where cancerous blood cells multiplied uncontrollably in her body. She was very sick and immunocompromised, and we were doing our best to support her on the journey. She spent months in and out of hospitals, clinics, and in our home-hospital room.

My first exposure to the world of digital health was during this time of great need. After months of inpatient care, chemotherapy, and a week-long ICU stay due to a treatment-induced heart condition, she was discharged home in mid-April to begin outpatient care. In an instant, we lost the 24/7 monitoring and access to a high level of hospital care. Set adrift on our own, we were forced to navigate a complex, comorbid care journey with limited face-to-face interaction with healthcare providers.

During the first peak of Covid-19 infections, I was tremendously thankful that we did not have to endure the tribulations of a complex leukemia care journey at the same time as a pandemic, where an infection would have added further complication to an already precarious clinical situation. At the same time, I felt the pain and the fear of those patients and family members fighting their own conditions during this time. With major disruption to inpatient and outpatient services and the risk of infection, adequate patient care was impossible.

Despite the widespread availability of digital tools, remote care technologies, telehealth, and other solutions in the market for years prior, our systems around the world were largely unprepared to manage patients when they were not physically located in a brick-and-mortar facility.

Realizing the immediate need and accelerating planned five-year digital transformation plans, health systems were forced to implement and adopt technologies. With new technologies being implemented in months rather than years, the digital health industry and virtual care models entered the mainstream.

But with great power and recognition also comes great responsibility for digital health companies, healthcare organizations, and policymakers moving forward. The power of virtual care and digital technologies in healthcare has not yet been realized. Beyond extending care remotely, these technologies have the potential to dramatically improve the effectiveness and experience for patients with chronic diseases like diabetes, hypertension, cancer, and depression.

* *

My journey into and passion for virtual care stems from my time as a caregiver for my mom during a particularly chaotic, complex, and traumatic journey through the US healthcare system. I was 20 years old, had just finished my emergency medical technician (EMT) training, and was in the middle of studying healthcare management and policy at Georgetown University. Everything I have done since then has been driven by a deep desire to build a better healthcare future for patients with chronic illnesses. The story begins at a local hospital in Atlanta, Georgia.

I pulled the car around to the patient discharge pickup location at Northside Hospital. Sitting outside in her wheelchair, in the shade under the awning, was my mom and a few members of our family. I parked the car and walked around the side to help her stand and move into the back seat carefully.

This was the first time in my life that I had to help my mom physically move anywhere. She was a marathon runner, a fifth-grade teacher, and a Tough Mudder. But, after nearly two months in the hospital, the former athlete and daily manager of 30 twelve-year-olds had lost weight and mobility and needed a wheelchair to move any distance greater than five or six feet.

Moving her was awkward at first but became more routine as she and I both began to accept the new dynamic between mother and son. The interpersonal part of the support in her movement was far more of a challenge than the technique for me, as I had recently completed my training as an EMT and was well versed in moving patients—nonetheless, they certainly do not teach caring for and coping with a very sick parent in EMT class.

After helping her get into the car, we began the hour-long journey home through rush hour traffic in Atlanta. For a newly discharged patient with leukemia, it was a challenging journey—and one we would be making frequently in the months after her first discharge from the bone marrow transplant floor.

She moved into the downstairs guest bedroom where a durable medical equipment provider had installed a hospital bed that we thought might make her caregiving and positioning easier now that she was back home. Instead of having 24-hour monitoring and supportive care provided by highly trained nurses and techs in the hospital, she was home and her care was now our responsibility. In the health system world, we call this period in a patient's journey the *post-acute* period.

According to the Medicare Payment Advisory Commission (MEDPAC), the definition of post-acute care is as follows:

> Post-acute care (PAC) includes rehabilitation or palliative services that [patients] receive after, or in some cases instead of, a stay in an acute care hospital. Depending on the intensity of care the patient requires, treatment may include a stay in a facility, ongoing outpatient therapy, or care provided at home.

MEDPAC is an organization that has been commissioned by the US Congress to monitor and analyze Medicare spending to recommend policies and needed changes to the Medicare Program.

The post-acute care area is one of the most expensive and crucial areas of innovation in healthcare. That's because it is a time of transition where previously critically ill patients are no longer being monitored by highly trained clinical staff. These transition points where the patient goes home are places where there is tremendous risk to health.

In this situation, my mom was in the hospital after intensive treatment for her chronic myeloid leukemia (CML). For the eight years prior to this hospitalization, she lived a relatively normal life aside from taking two pills a day, experiencing the side effects of those pills, and knowing that she was living with a dangerous disease.

In the years after her initial diagnosis, she was sent home with care plan instructions and a schedule to return for blood work on a semi-frequent basis. Her leukemia, in this situation, was in a chronic phase of the disease. Due to some phenomenal biomedical research on CML, the disease is managed with a unique class of small-molecule drug called tyrosine kinase inhibitors.

During this time, my mom was responsible for managing and ensuring that she followed her oncologist's instructions related to her condition. When not between the four walls of her physician's office, she was the sole responsible party for her own health and navigating her care journey.

Prior to her condition's precipitous decline that lead to this particular hospitalization, she lived those eight years with little official health support other than occasional oncologist visits. She, like other patients with a chronic disease, was left to her own devices between those office visits.

This model of care is consistent across many other chronic, or lifelong, conditions. Conditions like diabetes, various heart diseases, and autoimmune conditions are also managed in a similar manner. A patient goes to a physician, they receive a diagnosis, they receive a treatment plan, and then they are left to manage these conditions at home and with occasional 15-minute visits with a treating physician. In between those visits, there is an opportunity for things to go wrong.

We know this model does not work very well. As supported by our monumental spend on chronic illness in the US and across countries in the developed world, our model of chronic illness care is poor. In the US alone, we spend trillions on healthcare each year. In short, our spending is high while our health outcomes are poorer in the US compared to similar countries.

In 2018, the national healthcare expenditure (NHE) grew to $3.6 trillion, or $11,172 per person.[3] For perspective, that is 17.7% of our gross domestic product. And it's getting worse each year. The NHE is projected to grow at an average annual rate of 5.4% from 2019 through 2028, when it is expected to reach 6.2 trillion.

In a vacuum, these numbers mean very little when they are so big. Thus, it is important examine comparable countries like Germany, France, and the UK and the Organization for Economic Co-operation and Development (OECD) average (Table 1.1).

The table illustrates the significantly higher proportion of healthcare spending in the US compared to similar countries in the OECD. It is

TABLE 1.1

Health Spending in the US compared to OECD Countries (2018)

Country	Health Spending as Percentage of GDP (2018)
United States	17%
Germany	11%
France	11%
UK	10%
OECD Average	9%

important to note for later that, among the US and these other countries, a large portion of the expenditures are attributable to chronic illness. In the US, some estimates[4] suggest that about 75% of healthcare spending is linked to chronic illnesses like diabetes, musculoskeletal conditions, heart diseases, and cancers.

In the US and many other countries, healthcare spending is a crisis that is bankrupting citizens as they receive bills for services, in their role as taxpayers, and in their monthly insurance premiums. Given the poor performance, the US provides an important proving ground for innovations and policy measures that can be scaled and adopted by healthcare systems and organizations across the globe. Unsustainable healthcare spending is a problem, and its inflation in the US is likely attributable to a few important factors.

One, the US system is mix of public and private offerings without a universal coverage option. At any given time, approximately 10% to 15% of the population is without health insurance coverage, which results in costly episodes of care and a lack of access to preventive and needed healthcare services, like primary care. Other countries have some reliable means of public health coverage options and place a much larger emphasis on primary care services. This issue is compounded by poverty and socio-economic issues that accompany being uninsured.

Two, the US has higher healthcare prices for services than other countries. The for-profit element present in US healthcare leads to an effort to charge the highest price the market can bear. The segmentation of the healthcare market into payors and providers also encourages a lack of competition and price transparency. When you talk to biotechnology companies or health technology companies from other countries, they all seek to enter the US market, which represents the largest healthcare market in the world. US prices are high and this contributes to the large per capita healthcare spend[5].

Three, the way we pay for healthcare in the US incentivizes volume. We call this payment model fee-for-service (FFS). We pay healthcare organizations, physicians, hospitals, and other providers of care for each service provided. In order to maximize revenue under this model, hospitals want to fill beds, physicians want you in their office for appointments, and surgeons want to fill their schedules with procedures. Each one leads to more money, so the behavior of organizations in the system leads to increasing expenditures due to unnecessary care and a high volume of services.

Four, fraud, waste, and abuse (FWA) spending is expected to contribute to a significant portion of total spending on healthcare services. One estimate[6] suggests that as much as 30% of healthcare spending the US, in particular, is related to waste, inefficiencies, and those excessive prices. Pricing, FFS payment models, and waste all impact each other and drive increased spending per capita.

Five, our model of healthcare services fails to adequately care for patients with chronic illness. Our reactive and unsupportive model of care when patients are at home or in transition fails to lead to favorable health outcomes. This is due to both FFS incentives and the fragmented nature of healthcare services across the industry—there is poor communication and use of data. This, in turn, results in increased expenditures when patient conditions deteriorate and they end up receiving costly health services in the emergency department or hospitals. Chronic illnesses can often be both prevented and well managed. But our models of chronic disease care and lack of incentives for better care continue to produce bad outcomes for patients.

Thus, the following five areas are key foci for innovation efforts in the US:

- Lack of insurance coverage and access to healthcare
- The reduction of inflated prices
- Payment models: FFS to value-based care
- FWA
- Improved chronic care delivery models

Many of the present major reform movements in healthcare are focused on these five areas. For example, the concept of Medicare-for-All seeks to provide universal healthcare coverage, congressional efforts aimed at price transparency and drug pricing seek to reduce prices, new policies focused on changing how we pay for healthcare services seek to replace FFS payment models with value-based payment, and efforts to transform chronic care models seek to change the ways in which we provide care to patients living with our costliest conditions.

Each of these areas impacts the others. None exist in a vacuum. The focus of this book is on the improvement of chronic care delivery models using technology to improve the management of existing conditions and prevent future ones.

My thesis, when it comes to building a better, more effective healthcare system, is firmly rooted in the power and promise of digital technologies. Through these tools, the ways in which healthcare services meet the patient can be transformed from the existing episodic, in-person, and infrequent care models to something new and more effective.

Across the globe, the introduction of digital tools to clinical care delivery has and will continue to improve the efficiency and effectiveness of health services. Regardless of coverage systems, systemic prices, or payment models, clinical care delivery innovation has the potential to reach a large proportion of patients and can exist in a variety of political climates.

I maintain that in order for health services to become more effective we must look to the patient experience and the factors that affect health outcomes. This focus combined with the introduction of new technologies has the potential to unlock a healthier future. The patient is the end user of healthcare services, and anything that does not reflect a needed support is a system failure or wasteful component.

When we look more deeply at the patient experience with chronic illness care in the US, we see a very reactive system that fails to adequately support patients along their care journey. Chronic diseases are long-term issues, and thus the system must reflect that fact at a very basic level.

In time and politics, the variety of other efforts to develop some form of universal coverage, to manage hyperinflated prices, and to remove FFS payment models will yield fruit. However, in the meantime, the area of opportunity that addresses the models of care that touch the patient are the low-hanging fruit on our mission to improve health in the US and globally.

For the purpose of this book, I would like to offer the following thesis to you. If we are able to fundamentally alter the way we provide healthcare services to patients with chronic illness writ large, we will simultaneously reduce healthcare expenditures and improve population health and quality of life.

While this approach is very conceptual, I believe it is merited given the goal of healthcare systems across the globe to elevate the health of populations and entire societies. An investment in new, effective models of chronic disease care may fundamentally impact demand for healthcare services in the first place.

Part of this thesis is driven by the presupposition that patients who are healthy, or those with a stable condition, do not seek or require costly, intensive health services. Conceptually, an increase in the proportion of healthy and stable patients with chronic illness should result in a subsequent reduction in utilization of costly points of care like the emergency department or inpatient services. When effective models are scaled to more patients, the return on investment from this effect is realized.

Fortunately for us all, as we move into a more digitally immersed world, we are now forced to explore new innovations that can help us achieve this very outcome. The power of software and mobile technologies to connect people to information and healthcare providers is a new frontier for healthcare services.

* *

When we seek to drive positive impact for chronically ill patients, or any patient really, we need to look at what is being done for these patients on the ground. Too often, "innovations" are pursued in areas that may not reach patients or that do not fundamentally change the models of care that affect health outcomes. We cannot expect better health outcomes if we do nothing at the point of care to address patient needs and engagement.

Taking a step back, we can reduce most evidence-based chronic disease models to two basic activities that lead to value for patients: (1) actionable patient data collection and analysis and (2) effective and engaging communication between a provider of care and the patient.

These two activities are the basis for all interactions between healthcare provider and patient. While there are many subcategories and activities, these are the basic categorizations of "activities" that occur in healthcare services.

Models of care that perform these activities well are often more effective and of higher value in terms of patient outcomes.[7,8,9] Programs that perform well at these two activities are often deemed high-touch models of care. There is strong evidence that high-touch, high-frequency care for patients with chronic illness results in cost savings and improved health outcomes.[10,11,12] However, these models often face resistance at the organizational level due to potentially high costs and low return on investment (ROI)—especially in an FFS system. In fact, the most effective high-touch models of care are either extremely high-cost FFS service lines (e.g., my mom's hematology-oncology outpatient care) or operated in a full-risk payment model approach (e.g., organizations like ChenMed or Oak Street Health). But, there is a need to deliver engaging high-touch primary care in a scalable manner due to its effectiveness at driving positive health outcomes for patients with chronic disease.

It is often believed that the decision is between high-touch or high-tech care. But, in reality, technologies allow programs to cost-effectively operate high-touch models of care. The touches in this case might be virtual, but this approach enables an organization to operationalize and scale an effective high-touch program.

Due to the aforementioned systemic failures, specifically the FFS payment model, current chronic care has been reduced to infrequent, 15-minute episodes of care that rely on a model that only looks only at physiological processes of disease rather than other health-impacting factors (e.g., lifestyle, environmental, and socioeconomic factors.) The current models treat patient health as cross-sectional rather than longitudinal and do not view health as holistically established by health science.

From the patient perspective, *health* is always. Patients live with and manage their condition in real time, 24/7, 365 days a year. When patients are in the home or their communities, they are left on their own to manage their conditions with little support from healthcare providers. This might be fine if enough time is spent teaching patients to successfully manage and understand their conditions, but we know that this does not happen at a sufficient scale. Time, then, is a major limitation in the current US health system.

Patients also do not have access to their own health data. How does a patient, who is expected to self-manage at home, know they are on the right path to health? How can they track their performance? How can they advocate for themselves when they are unable to measure their own health status? Thus, patient data is also not leveraged as a tool to enable patients to self-manage their condition.

In order to build modern, advanced chronic care models, it is time to think outside the historical healthcare box. It is time to apply the knowledge from health sciences, medicine, and public health to truly address the root causes of bad health. It is time to leverage ubiquitous technologies to improve communication and data collection. It is time to extend high-touch models of care to patients with chronic illness to produce better health and lower costs. It is time to empower patients with their own health data so they can become true partners in their pursuit of better health. It is time to rethink the need for healthcare to be provided in a brick-and-mortar facility.

The first two decades of the 21st century have been wrought with technological advancement at an exponential pace. With it has come a particular tool that has the potential to transform modern healthcare systems: The smartphone.

NOTES

1. Ateev Mehrotra et al. "The Impact of the COVID-19 Pandemic on Outpatient Visits: A Rebound Emerges." To the Point (blog), Commonwealth Fund, May 19, 2020. https://doi.org/10.26099/ds9e-jm36
2. Bradley Fox and Owen Sizemore. "Epic Health Research Network." 2020. Online. www.ehrn.org/telehealth-fad-or-the-future/
3. National Health Expenditure Data. "Centers for Medicare and Medicaid Services." Accessed 2020. Online. www.cms.gov/Research-Statistics-Data-and-Systems/Statis tics-Trends-and-Reports/NationalHealthExpendData/NationalHealthAccounts Historical
4. V. J. Dzau, M. B. McClellan, J. M. McGinnis, S. P. Burke, M. J. Coye, A. Diaz . . . E. Zerhouni. "Vital Directions for Health and Health Care." *JAMA*, 317(14) (2017): 1461. https://doi.org/10.1001/jama.2017.1964
5. Gerard F. Anderson, Peter Hussey, and Varduhi Petrosyan. "It's Still The Prices, Stupid: Why The US Spends So Much On Health Care, and a Tribute To Uwe Reinhardt." *Health Affairs*, 38(1) (2019): 87–95. https://doi.org/10.1377/hlthaff. 2018.05144.
6. V. J. Dzau, M. B. McClellan, J. M. McGinnis, et al. "Vital Directions for Health and Health Care: Priorities From a National Academy of Medicine Initiative." *JAMA*, 317(14) (2017): 1461–1470. https://doi.org/10.1001/jama.2017.1964
7. Rainer S. Beck, Rebecca Daughtridge, and Philip D. Sloane. "Physician-Patient Communication in the Primary Care Office: A Systematic Review." *Journal of the American Board of Family Practice,* 15(1) (2002): 25–38.
8. R. Ghany, L. Tamariz, G. Chen, E. Dawkins, A. Ghany, E. Forbes, and T. Tajiri. "High-Touch Care Leads to Better Outcomes and Lower Costs in a Senior Population." *American Journal of Managed Care*, 24(9) (2018): e300–304.
9. Jeanne M. Ferrante, Bijal A. Balasubramanian, Shawna V. Hudson, and Benjamin F. Crabtree. "Principles of the Patient-Centered Medical Home and Preventive Services Delivery." *Annals of Family Medicine,* 8(2) (2010): 108–116. https://doi. org/10.1370/afm.1080.
10. Ibid., 8.
11. Ibid., 9.
12. Craig Tanio, and Christopher Chen. "Innovations at Miami Practice Show Promise for Treating High-Risk Medicare Patients." *Health Affairs,* 32(6) (2013): 1078–1082. https://doi.org/10.1377/hlthaff.2012.0201.

2

Digital Health—A New Industry

The time after my mom got home from her inpatient stay was full of new challenges. We were responsible for providing the same or a similar level of care that was previously provided by trained professionals in the hospital. Her activities of daily living and medical care were complex processes that required a number of steps throughout the day. Despite a dedicated group of caregivers with healthcare experience, it was clear as soon as we got home—we were on our own.

We used a pink binder to track and record medication administration, weight, vital signs, meals, and many other processes. We tracked appointments on a paper calendar and kept her lab results in hard copy in the inside cover of the binder.

We collected and analyzed her vitals and symptoms to better understand how her condition was improving or deteriorating. Our data set was distinct and separate from the clinical data used by her hematology clinic. Data was only shared and collected at in-person office visits. We were not asked about her blood pressure trends over the last two weeks, nor were we asked about her weight trends at home. They collected a snapshot of vitals in the office but neglected to piece together a longitudinal record of key clinical metrics related to my mom's condition.

The uncertainty, in our minds, as we navigated her care journey at home, was the worst part. When not in the clinic, we had little communication with her care team. It was either a phone call to leave a message after hours, a visit to the emergency department, or nothing. As a very "healthcare-literate" family, we knew to collect data, research information on her condition through reliable sources, and communicate irregularities to her providers when given the opportunity during the in-person outpatient visits. We also knew how to mitigate potential risk factors for bad outcomes.

Many patients and caregivers are not as privileged and healthcare-literate, and many more do not naturally collect or act on data. Low health literacy in patients is associated with the following impactful outcomes: poor adherence to established care plans, difficulty understanding the complexity of one's own health, a general lack of knowledge about health and health services, difficulty comprehending health instructions, low recognition and understanding of preventive services, generally poorer health, and the potential for earlier death.[1]

A large proportion of patients relies solely on the occasional guidance of their care teams to navigate their chronic care health journeys. The current models of care for patients with a chronic illness are based around this infrequent, in-person care that leaves much to be desired in between visits.

We are reaching a point in the United States where the current system is unsustainable for the reasons previous mentioned but, most importantly, because the current models of care delivery do not reflect the needs of the patient and fail to produce positive health outcomes at scale. The problems with US healthcare, in particular, are well defined and well known in the industry—yet change and substantial improvement have failed to scale.

Thousands of programs and innovation efforts have been conceptualized, implemented, and studied to solve these very same problems. Many of the core issues in health services can be distilled down to failures of data use and communication. Due to this, some of the most promising innovations on the horizon are based around the power of the smartphone.

Since the advent and diffusion of these new technologies across populations globally, innovators have recognized the potential benefit of smartphones to solve some of these key data and communication issues faced by health systems, healthcare providers and, most importantly, patients.

Through innovative pilots at health systems, academic medical centers, private companies, and Silicon Valley start-ups, people have been working for the last two decades to use smartphones and mobile devices to facilitate better care to patients in the home and in their communities, care that is more reflective and supportive of the longitudinal patient journeys and that prioritizes personalized patient engagement. To ameliorate the effects of poor health literacy, smartphones and new care models can enable healthcare providers to provide a high-touch level of support for patients to proactively promote health and prevent disease.

These innovation efforts have begun to take hold. Instead of using pink binders to record vitals, patients are receiving smartphone apps. Instead of flagging irregularities picked up by chance medical knowledge or caregiver diligence, apps can communicate automatically to a patient or alert a healthcare provider of potential issues. Instead of data being locked in a clinic's electronic health record, patients have access to their own health metrics on their phone.

The innovators, technologists, companies, and clinical program developers that have led the charge for the smartphone's injection into healthcare have begun to fall under the broad categorization of *digital health*, or the *health tech*, industry.

A DEFINITIONAL ISSUE

The digital health industry is full of buzzwords, terminology, and creative marketing phrases. The terms *digital health, health tech, telehealth, telemedicine, remote-patient monitoring (RPM), virtual care, mHealth, iHealth, e-health, connected care, digital therapeutics*, and others are used to describe the health technologies, companies, and clinical models that are powered by digital and mobile technologies.

Some call it an industry, while others might call it a movement. The digital health movement, then, is the push to utilize digital technologies to enhance healthcare services. As with anything new, there exists a major definition problem as made clear by the number of terms that are frequently utilized within and about the industry. For example, telehealth and telemedicine are largely used interchangeably. Connected care and virtual care are terms often used by different people to describe the same models of care.

The Health Information Management Systems Society defines digital health as follows:

> Digital health connects and empowers people and populations to manage health and wellness, augmented by accessible and supportive provider teams working within flexible, integrated, interoperable and digitally-enabled

care environments that strategically leverage digital tools, technologies and services to transform care delivery.

Digital health and health tech are the terms that typically refer to the movement, the industry, and the groups of companies that operate within it. These companies or healthcare organizations, unsurprisingly, rely on or provide digital technologies that augment healthcare services.

For the sake of this book, I will use digital health or health tech to refer to the space and technologies as a whole. The following additional definitions[2] will be utilized for the purpose of this book to ensure clarity:

Virtual care: A model of care that utilizes digital communications technology to provide care to patients not physically located in the same location as the healthcare provider or care team. This is a broad term that refers to a clinical model. Typically, this is the antithesis of face-to-face care.

Connected care: A model of care that typically utilizes communications technology to provide care to patients over a period of time. Connected care models seek to bridge the gap between when patients are in-person and when they are outside of the four walls of a healthcare facility. This model typically utilizes digital technologies to ensure that patients have access to their care teams consistently over time. Specifically, this term may refer to a model of care that emphasizes patient relationships and engagement with a care team through the use of technology.

mHealth: Shorthand for *mobile health*. This is a broad category that typically refers to the technologies and systems that rely on mobile electronic devices and networks to impact health. A smartphone application used in a virtual care model is an example of mHealth.

Digital therapeutics: A category of clinical interventions that are typically prescription-based. As opposed to the prescription of a pharmaceutical product, digital therapeutics are digital technologies that are US Food and Drug Administration (FDA)-approved to treat a specific disease or condition. The distinction here is the FDA approval and prescription components.

Remote-patient monitoring (RPM): A model of care that involves the collection of physiological or clinically relevant metrics from patients when they are not physically located in the monitoring healthcare facility. Broadly, RPM programs utilize medical devices or mobile applications to transmit real-time clinical data to a healthcare provider to enable response to a condition or to gather more insight into patient health stats outside the office. This term is used both as a concept and a clearly defined program by CMS.

Telemedicine[3]: The provision of medical services through a technology like a telephone, audio-visual technologies, or asynchronous messaging. Telemedicine is one of the first "digital health" models. Telemedicine is often used to broadly describe the industry, but the term itself refers to the rendering of medical services, by a licensed medical provider, to patients remotely.

Telehealth: The provision of healthcare services to patients via a technology like telephone, audio-visual technologies, or asynchronous messaging. The distinction from telemedicine is the use of the term "health" rather than "medicine" which has a broader categorization and that represents a wider range of disciplines including but not limited to medicine. Health may involve care providers who are not physicians or those trained in medicine and may utilize clinical interventions that reside outside of the typical medical model.

e-Health: An older term that refers to the use of internet and other computer technologies in health services or for a health purpose. Mostly used by old stuffy academics in older papers and occasionally in new ones.

Regardless of the term, all of these refer to either groups of technologies or the delivery or augmentation of healthcare services through the use of digital technologies, often accessed through a smartphone or via an internet-accessing device. You will notice that I use virtual care and RPM most frequently unless talking about historic roots.

*

The digital health industry has experienced both tremendous growth and increasing interest among investors, traditional healthcare organizations, and patients. According to Rock Health, in 2019, $8.9 billion was invested in digital health companies by venture capital firms. As of the third quarter of 2020, during the height of the Covid-19 pandemic, $9.4 billion dollars was invested in digital health innovation,[4] illustrating a significant growth from the year prior.

Why is this happening? Here are seven major drivers of this effect:

1. Digital transformation has already hit other industries hard, and healthcare is lagging far behind—patients desire a digital experience.
2. Patient outcomes and experience with care has been poor, and thus innovation is required.
3. Healthcare costs are out of control, and thus new payment models and efforts to control spending are driving technology innovation.
4. A wider understanding of the drivers of health outcomes are prompting new models of care to be explored.
5. Healthcare professionals are burning out in the current models and increasingly seek new ways to perform their jobs.
6. The growth in the software engineering workforce and the growth of cloud-based technologies has democratized skills and reduced the cost to enter a market.
7. The Covid-19 pandemic forced healthcare organizations to adopt digital technologies to deliver care as face-to-face services became too risky. Patients, in turn, were exposed to a new way to receive services.

IMPROVING THE PATIENT EXPERIENCE: A UNIVERSAL EXPERIENCE

If you think about your most recent healthcare experience, you probably had to make a trip to the office via some mode of transportation—maybe you drove or took public transportation. Then you may have spent considerable time in a waiting room despite having an appointment. You may have filled out the same paper forms and used your hard-copy insurance card for payment. You may have two separate doctors who fax records to each other or do not communicate at all prior to your visit. Before even seeing a healthcare provider you have already sunk a good deal of time into the process.

Once you get into the exam room, your healthcare provider may ask you questions about how you are feeling, your lifestyle, your medications, and your diet and may perform bloodwork or other tests. All this information is recorded in a format that may be paper or electronic. Once it is recorded, it is up to your healthcare provider to analyze the information to produce a diagnosis or treatment plan.

Your 15 minutes with that provider and hour of waiting does not feel like a good use of your time, and you likely do not have a better handle on your health once it's all over. This is especially concerning if you have been having troubling symptoms or are living with a long-term chronic illness.

Upon completion of all the tests and the screening questions, you may be sent home to wait for a call or asked to return to the office for a follow-up. You also may be diagnosed in the office if results are available fast enough. Either way, you and your healthcare provider will eventually arrive at either a clean bill of health, a result showing no change, or a care plan for treatment.

In that 15-minute meeting with your healthcare provider, you may not understand what is going on, and you may have questions about your health. You may be worried that things aren't getting better and you have no way to know whether what you are doing is working because you have no data available on your health at home. You are confused, concerned for your health, and unable to fully meet the goals of the treatment plan. Sometimes, you do not even speak or read English very well and the materials are difficult to understand.

Your care plan likely includes some form of medication, lifestyle changes, an exercise regimen, physical therapy, and/or dietary changes. It may be communicated to you verbally, or it may be handed to you on a piece of paper. You then leave the office, pick up your prescriptions, and must navigate your new diagnosis and care on your own until the next appointment—which may be a few months away. Your prescription may have gotten lost on the way to the pharmacy. Thus, you take to the internet to learn more about your condition or, like many patients, you just return to your normal life while attempting to follow the instructions that you received two months ago and do not understand.

You may have received new medications to add to your daily list. Medications are the cornerstone of treatment for many conditions, but they are also dangerous due to their significant impact on body systems.[5] Your physician may not have checked your entire medication list despite the importance of a thorough medication review—they may not have time because they get paid per visit and need to fit more into each day to maintain financial viability.

Many digital health companies are attempting to make this experience better, easier, and faster as well as more effective at supporting patients toward stable health.

Digital health, as a broad sector, seeks to enhance administrative tools, clinical tools, and patient interaction to make the healthcare experience more effective, efficient, and positive for patients. Healthcare is far behind in the adoption of digital technology, and the digital health industry is looking to fill that gap. Besides the obvious clinical drivers, healthcare is also being pushed toward digital due to rapid adoption and positive customer experiences created by other industries. The growth of fintech for finance, ecommerce for retail, and online streaming services for media has affected perceptions of healthcare services.

DIGITAL EXPERIENCES AND CONSUMER DESIRES

One of the best examples of the power of digitization in other industries can be seen in media and entertainment. Media and entertainment companies quickly adopted digital technologies and digital-centric business models. The transition from brick-and-mortar or hard-copy customer experiences in the industry occurred quickly. The story of Blockbuster Video perfectly illustrates the concept.

I remember taking trips to Blockbuster with my dad on an almost weekly basis. We would peruse the stacks of hard-copy DVDs that were available and pick up a few to take home. Instead of waiting for the TV Guide to indicate a specific movie was on the horizon, you could go to the brick-and-mortar store and get one, on demand.

While this concept is now foreign to us and to many in younger generations, it was not too long ago that this was the way we consumed movies and other entertainment. Then, the digital transformation began and Blockbuster began to encounter stiff competition that was deeply focused on transforming the customer experience. That competition was Netflix. First, Netflix took a step closer to our homes through the availability of movies shipped through the mail and ordered via web-based digital interface. It was faster, it was easier, and it provided a wider selection. Through a novel digital experience, the innovation quickly made the physical trip to a Blockbuster obsolete.

The story did not stop there. Netflix continued to evolve in a manner that relied even more heavily on digital experience. Soon, rather than shipping hard-copy DVDs, Netflix allowed consumers to stream movies directly into the home via their smartphones, computers, and internet-enabled televisions. This was the nail in the coffin for Blockbuster as digitally delivered and consumed movies became dominant.

Now, a full technology giant, Netflix dominates the media and entertainment industry, with 167.1 million subscribers[6] as of 2019. Blockbuster, on the other hand, has one store remaining in Bend, Oregon. The failure to adapt to the emerging digital technology trends led Blockbuster to complete failure and Netflix to industry-defining domination.

***

Just like Netflix slowly walked into the home using digital and mobile technology, so will healthcare services. Digital health companies and healthcare organizations adopting a digital-front-door strategy are both looking to transform some aspects of healthcare into an experience that is closer to that of Netflix. Healthcare deals with disease, suffering, and quality of life rather than movies, so the transformation will be different, but the very importance of healthcare services underscores the need to continue developing more effective and satisfactory models of care delivery.

Digital health companies desire to give patients access to healthcare providers via video conference on a mobile phone—that's *telehealth, telemedicine, or virtual care*. Some companies want to enhance the patient appointment scheduling experience by enabling features on an app or online rather than exclusively over the phone. Others want to provide lab results and tests through an app quickly and more understandably rather than via paper received at an in-person visit. Even more want to bring the entirety of certain health services into the hands of the consumer via the smartphone. Instead of waiting in a physical waiting room for hours, a digital experience may be available on demand in a patient's living room.

The digital health movement is all about creating convenient patient experiences, better health outcomes, improved access to care, and increased efficiency in clinical programs all through the power of digital tools. The holy grail of the digital health industry is improved patient health outcomes at a lower cost.

Our smartphones sit in our pockets or are nearby at all times, just as our health is with us at all times. Thus, the use of the smartphone to complement the monitoring and improvement of health makes sense either as a stand-alone tool or as a medium to facilitate better connection between healthcare providers and their patients.

It is not a matter of *whether* it happens; it is a matter of how fast this revolution will occur in healthcare and what it looks like on the other side. It is essential that adopters stick to the evidence and avoid the hype.

NOTES

1. Roundtable on Health Literacy; Board on Population Health and Public Health Practice; Institute of Medicine. Health Literacy: Improving Health, Health Systems, and Health Policy Around the World: Workshop Summary. Washington (DC): National Academies Press (US); 2013 July 10. Appendix A, Health Literacy Around the World: Part 1 Health Literacy Efforts Outside of the United States.
2. Note: I do use many of these interchangeably throughout the book to prevent too much repetition.
3. I am generally against the use of the term "telemedicine" due to the physician-centricity of it. We have a wide range of providers for virtual care, and thus I believe telehealth or virtual care are more appropriate. If care is delivered via a physician, then, sure, let's call it telemedicine in that instance, but not to describe any model of care facilitated by technology.
4. Elaine Wang, and Sean Day. "Q3 2020: A New Annual Record for Digital Health, Data from the Rock Health Funding Database. 2020. https://rockhealth.com/reports/q3-2020-digital-health-funding-already-sets-a-new-annual-record/
5. Medication-centered treatment is also a product of medicine's, as an institution, inability or unwillingness to incorporate the biopsychosocial model into practice. Individual behavior, nutrition, socioeconomic factors, and environmental factors are equally as, or more, important to address when seeking to improve health. Medications alter physiological processes but do not address lifestyle or socioeconomic factors of disease.
6. Reported by Netflix in 2019.

3

The Smartphone and the Internet

I grew up at the very tail end of the Millennial generation and the very beginning of Gen Z. Collectively, we are a strange group because we grew up in a very analog and non-digital world, but we fully witnessed the rapid transformation to digital. I witnessed the complete transition from floppy discs to DVDs to streaming and the entire evolution from flip phones through the very first smartphones. My age group is not filled with digital natives, but rather digital pioneers. We remember a time before smartphones, Wi-Fi, and Netflix.

When I was in sixth grade, my best friend Charlie called me on my Samsung Glide phone to tell me about this new service from Dell he had just discovered—Dell Video Chat. The very next day, I begged my Dad to take me to Target so I could buy a webcam to hook up to my laptop in order to video chat with Charlie via Dell Video Chat. This was my first experience with very early capabilities of synchronous audio/visual signals transmitted over the internet in real time. I remember being incredibly excited about this innovation—the potential seemed limitless.

Today, audio-visual communication technologies like Apple's FaceTime and Zoom are ubiquitous. Just like millions of others, I spend hours of my life on Zoom calls each day. The technology enables people to work from anywhere and to collaborate with colleagues around the world. With applications like FaceTime, friends and family are a few screen-touches away. As internet networks (e.g., 3G, 4G, and 5G), Wi-Fi, and smartphones took the world by storm, societies changed remarkably.

The digital world has become more and more accessible and powerful. It has impacted essentially all industries, people, and even animals as organizations and individuals have built their online presence. It quickly became clear that the use cases are endless. Driving the digital revolution, two primary innovations have shepherded the digital health industry: the internet and the smartphone. Without these two inventions, there would be no digital health efforts to undertake.

Expanding on the first iteration of the internet, broadband wireless internet access both in homes and through direct wireless connections to smartphones has further expanded the use and potential for these technologies. The power to transmit data, media, and communications in milliseconds across the globe has transformed human society. Smartphones have provided computer processing capabilities and endless information directly into the home and the hands, or pockets, of millions of people.

INTERNET AND SMARTPHONES: A GLOBAL PERSPECTIVE

The internet has been one of humanity's most transformational and exponential technologies. Globally, the number of internet users increased rapidly from just around 413 million in 2000 to over 3.4 billion in 2016.[1] In 2005, the 1 billion user milestone was achieved. From 2011 to 2016, each day saw an average of 640,000 people who gained access to the internet for the first time.[2]

Looking at data[3] compiled by Max Roser and colleagues in 2015, with respect to internet use across the globe, China and India take the top two slots in terms of total internet users despite having only 50% and 26% of their populations online, respectively. The top six countries by number of internet users in 2016 were:

China = 765 million
India = 391 million
United States = 245 million
Brazil = 126 million
Japan = 116 million
Russia = 109 million

In a similar manner to the internet, mobile technology has also spread exponentially around the globe. In 2018, it was estimated that approximately 5 billion people owned mobile devices.[4] Of those mobile devices, somewhere over half are smartphones.[5] Despite the large ownership numbers in aggregate, the growth in mobile technology to date has not been uniform across countries or across populations within them.

People in advanced economies are more likely both to own a smartphone and to have access to the internet than those people in emerging economies. For example, a median of 76% of the population across 18 advanced economies surveyed have smartphones, compared with a median of only 45% of people in emerging economies.[6] This inequity can be seen as cause for concern, but the numbers are still remarkably high and represent a major opportunity for health services from global and domestic perspectives.

The inter- and intra-country expansion of both internet access and smartphone ownership has led to an explosion of innovation. Healthcare has been no different. Globally, the promise of digital health quickly meant the efficient provision of healthcare services and expertise to remote areas or those geographic areas that are medically underresourced. As internet and devices reach increasingly remote areas, this promise is realized. Once access is achieved, the opportunities for use case expansion are vast.

The internet expansion to the developing world, in the global healthcare community, has tremendously improved capabilities and reach for innovative healthcare organizations and nongovernmental organizations. This is likely one of the most significant impacts of the digital health revolution, and it is one that I am far too underqualified to discuss in detail. It is important to note that the gains in healthcare quality and access to medical care driven by the use of digitally delivered health services in areas of the developing world should not be understated.

THE INTERNET: THE US PERSPECTIVE

My focus has been on the healthcare system of the United States and, by extension, those of the developed world that share similar clinical institutions and regimes. Among these health systems, the United States performs relatively worse. But, the internet is well suited to help drive significant change moving forward. Indeed, the digital health revolution will help solve some of the serious gaps in the US health system as they relate to the programs that actually drive patient benefit.

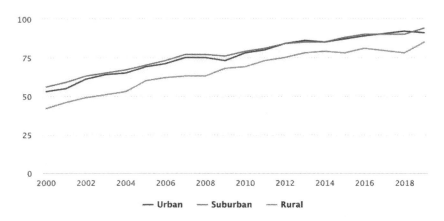

FIGURE 3.1
Percentage of US Adults Who Use the Internet, by Community Type.

After all, good healthcare is often as much about patient education, communication, and engagement as it is about anything else. This is one aspect of the internet that we know works exceptionally well when done properly. To better understand the digital health movement and its place in the future of healthcare, it is important to establish an understanding of the current internet and smartphone trends.

In the United States, the internet expansion has been closely measured by Pew Research Centers.[7] In Figure 3.1, the growth in US adults who use the internet rose sharply from approximately 50% in the year 2000 to greater than 80% in 2018.

The same chart also shows the differences across urban, suburban, and rural geographies. Urban and suburban areas have a consistently greater percentage of adults who use the internet than rural areas, but the growth has been consistent across all three communities.

Rural Areas

Despite steady growth over the last two decades, rural areas still lag behind urban and suburban areas with respect to internet usage. This is particularly applicable to healthcare discussions surrounding the use of digital technologies due to the promise of improved access in areas with limited physical healthcare service locations.

Individuals who reside in rural areas tend to have a low supply of healthcare providers and often must travel a longer distance to reach them.[8] Rural areas have historically poorer access to healthcare services across specialties.[9] In a similar trend, evidence suggests that children in rural areas are less likely to receive advice about a healthy diet, exercise, and the risks of smoking than are children in urban areas.[10] Overall, hospitals located in rural areas have more complex and sicker patients than those facilities in urban areas.[11] In addition, many of these key disparities between rural and urban areas increase in magnitude for individuals who are African American or Hispanic.

As a general rule, populations in rural areas are more likely to be older, poorer, sicker, and uninsured.[12] They also have higher rates of opioid use disorder, injury, smoking, and suicide. Life expectancy is often used to compare the health of populations between geographic areas. Over time, the life expectancy in rural areas has gone down at a faster rate than that of many urban areas overall.[13] It is important to mention here that within urban areas, there also exist wide disparities in life expectancy, where one zip code can show a significantly lower life expectancy than a nearby zip code.

Older Adults

When thinking about a population that has high rates of chronic illness and that can benefit from technology, the first that comes to mind is older adults. Older adults represent a higher proportion of the population in rural areas and experience a high prevalence of chronic illnesses associated with aging. Older adults also often experience mobility issues and challenges with their activities of daily living.[14] As much of the global population ages, this core group of societal elders will become an increasingly important group for healthcare and social service systems.

With decreased mobility comes difficulty accessing needed healthcare services. A higher risk for chronic illnesses coupled with this difficulty accessing services leads to a population at risk for bad health outcomes and costly episodes of care.

One of the biggest critiques of the digital health industry is the perceived inability for older adults to access and use the technologies in their care. However, the data tells another story, one that is rapidly changing.

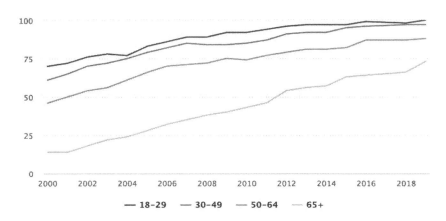

FIGURE 3.2
Percentage of US Adults Who Use the Internet, by Age.

In Figure 3.2, again from Pew Research data, the percentage of adults who report using the internet is shown from the year 2000 until 2018.[15] Adults older than 65 have progressed from a reported usage at well below 25% in 2002 to close to 75% internet use. The entire population, in fact, is converging quickly on 100% utilization at the current rates, as approximately 10,000 people turn 65 each day in the United States. Thus, those individuals in younger age groups continue to bring their internet use and smartphone ownership into US Medicare eligibility.

The benefits of using digital technology to deliver healthcare, for older adults, are numerous. Given the increased access to and adoption of the internet within this population, the potential exists to solve some important problems associated with an aging populace.

For older adults with mobility issues or those geographically distant from a physical healthcare provider, the delivery of health services and check-ins over the internet offers a convenient and accessible alternative to face-to-face care.

Similarly, the delivery of services via the internet can also allow for more touchpoints with older adults who already experience loneliness at higher rates than other age groups. Older adults often report that their visit to their doctor is one of their main social interaction opportunities. Thus, the replacement of in-person care is not reasonable, but rather the addition of new virtual touchpoints or the use of virtual care when physical care is not possible can provide social interaction opportunities for older patients.

Importantly, digital tools can be specially designed for the use of older adults to improve usability and engagement. Some companies in digital health have built specially designed applications and tablets to improve visibility and in-app navigation for older adults.

It is clear, however, that as we continue to move into the next 20 years of healthcare transformation, internet access rates will continue to improve for all age groups, enabling the continued growth of digital health models.

THE SMARTPHONE

According to the Cambridge Dictionary,[16] a smartphone is a cell phone that can be used as a small computer and that connects to the internet.

Just as the internet network continues to spread through the population, across geographic areas, into the home, and into the pockets of millions of people, so did the computer. Together with the internet, this trend has also set the stage for the digital health movement.

I grew up with a flip phone during the time that the Motorola Razr was the coolest phone on the market. Cell phone technology grew up right before our eyes during the early 2000s. After my first flip phone, I graduated to one of the first touch screen phones available, the Samsung Glyde. It was a poorly functioning and comparatively small screen accompanied by a slide out, horizontal, full keyboard that was still needed to use the SMS-text function due to the limitations of the touch screen.

The first iPhone commercial began running on television in mid-2007, and I vividly remember seeing it for the first time. It was striking. The functionality, the modernity, and its limitless potential were clear. Apparently, it became clear to everyone else as well because the smartphone market exploded quickly in the years after.

Pew Research Center collects information on cell phone use, and it was not until about 2011 that they included smartphones in the survey. But, the data shown in the Figure 3.3 is still telling of the impact smartphones have had on US society.

From a rate of ownership hovering just above ~30% in 2011, smartphone ownership rates climbed to above 75% of the US population in 2018. The

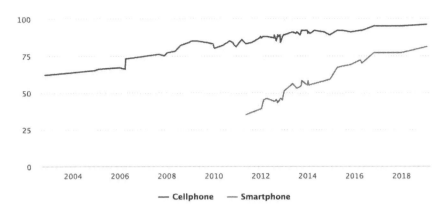

FIGURE 3.3
Percentage of US Adults Who Own Smartphones and Cell Phones.

high rate of adoption has prompted a rush to develop applications and tools for these pocket computers that accompany their owners in most situations. Apps have hit the market for thousands of use cases, with health being a chief pursuit among developers.

The power of the smartphone for use in healthcare resides in three concepts: the ability to transmit data and information, the ability to facilitate communication between the owner and healthcare service providers, and the fact that the phone is never too far from its owner.

Health is with a person at all times, and so too is the smartphone. It is this concept plus the technical capabilities of the phone–internet complex that provides the scaffold on which healthcare services can more effectively impact health.

Smartphones and the Internet: Population Segments

Digital health services and programs require the use of an expensive smartphone and continuous internet access. Thus, one of the primary criticisms aimed at the digital health movement are concerns about equity.[17] Will the growth and expansion of healthcare solutions delivered via smartphone leave people behind who cannot afford smartphones? Will access go only to the wealthy? Will the widespread use lead to a two-tiered system of healthcare with one for the poor and one with technology for the rich? Will rural areas with comparatively lower rates of smartphone ownership and internet use be left behind further? These are all questions that must be answered and addressed by the industry in conjunction with both state and federal policymakers moving forward.

The same Pew Research Center data[18] further provides insights into the distribution of smartphone ownership across the US population. In total, 81% of the population reports owning a smartphone. In Table 3.1, smartphone ownership is evaluated across a number of demographic, socioeconomic, and geographic categories. There are several relevant conclusions to be drawn.

First, most people have some form of cell phone. Even in the 65+ age group, 91% have either a smartphone or a non-smartphone cell phone.

TABLE 3.1

Distribution of Smartphone and Cell Phone Ownership, by Category

	Any cellphone	Smartphone	Cellphone, but not smartphone
Total	96%	81%	15%
Men	98%	84%	14%
Women	95%	79%	16%
Ages 18–29	99%	96%	4%
30–49	99%	92%	6%
50–64	95%	79%	17%
65+	91%	53%	39%
White	96%	82%	14%
Black	98%	80%	17%
Hispanic	96%	79%	17%
Less than high school graduate	92%	66%	25%
High school graduate	96%	72%	24%
Some college	96%	85%	11%
College graduate	98%	91%	7%
Less than $30,000	95%	71%	23%
$30,000–$49,999	96%	78%	18%
$50,000–$74,999	98%	90%	8%
$75,000+	100%	95%	5%
Urban	97%	83%	13%
Suburban	96%	83%	13%
Rural	95%	71%	24%

Source: Survey conducted January 8 to February 7, 2019.

This is the category with the lowest number reported for that column. Thus, engagement with all ages, areas, and demographics is possible via voice transmission or SMS-text—and many health technology companies are building programs designed to use this more basic technology to better engage patients who may not have or easily use a smartphone. While the functionality may be less rich than a program delivered via smartphone, the engagement and communication capabilities are still available.

Second, with respect to income, there is a disparity in smartphone ownership between the wealthy (95%) and those of low income (71%). While only 5% of people making more than $75,000 do not have a smartphone, 29% of people making less than $30,000 a year report not having a smartphone device. Thus, folks with lower incomes are at a technological disadvantage. This is the root of the argument that digital health has an equity problem.

Third, looking at race and ethnicity, disparities appear smaller than those seen when segmenting the population by income. Among white people, 82% report having a smartphone, while the Black and Hispanic segments of the population report 80% and 79%, respectively.

Fourth, just like with internet access, there is a disparity between urban/suburban communities (83%) and rural (71%) ones with respect to smartphone ownership. This is a major limitation when it comes to the goal of extending health services to locations with geographic access issues to face-to-face health services. But, taking a glass half-full approach, it is promising to see the rates of both internet access and smartphone ownership consistently growing in rural areas. For those with both internet access and a device, the delivery of digitally augmented healthcare services is possible.

Fifth, education level segmentation shows a disparity between more highly educated people and those with less than a high school education. Those with a college degree have a 91% smartphone ownership rate, whereas those with less than a high school education report 66% ownership. This effect is likely due to income driven by education differences rather than inherent differences due to the education itself. Many of the differences seen here within other categories may be a result of income differences rather than the effect of the segment itself. Smartphones are comparatively expensive compared to non-smartphone cell phones.

Finally, with respect to age group differences, the data shows that people aged 18 to 29 have the highest rate of smartphone ownership, while older adults aged 65+ have a much lower rate of smartphone ownership, at 53%.

Many older adults utilize a desktop computer to access the internet and therefore may be able to access digitally delivered health services via a computer. However, it is my opinion that 53% is a strong number that supports the idea that the unique advantages of these digital models can be conferred to many older adults; rates of ownership are also increasing.

A Note About Equity and Disparities

I would be remiss if I failed to highlight and specifically address the current disparities and inequities that exist in healthcare and in health outcomes among racial groups. I took a positive lens when evaluating the current state of internet access and smartphone ownership to suggest that the current increasing trends and rates of ownership are positive for digital health's ability to meet patients across a wide variety of demographics.

However, health disparities are rampant in healthcare. The Pew data illustrates a similar story to the disparities seen in health outcomes. Lower-income, rural, older, Black, and Hispanic populations have lower rates of smartphone ownership and internet access than wealthier, white, urban, and younger populations. This divide exists in health outcomes across a wide variety of measures. For example, rural areas have higher rates of chronic illness than suburban areas, Black mothers have higher rates of maternal mortality than white mothers, and older adults have higher rates of loneliness than younger populations.

While the rates of smartphone ownership and broadband internet access across all demographics are improving, it will be important to monitor disparities created due to the provision of healthcare services via digital tools. If digital health companies and virtual care delivery models are built to improve health outcomes, then the very people who need them most may not have sufficient access. This possibility should not be ignored, and proactive steps to ensure access should be taken by companies and the greater healthcare ecosystem.

Virtual care models and digital health companies have emerged as solutions to some of healthcare's most crucial issues to address. Any disparities resulting from their use would represent a failure to deliver on promises. This represents an important area for collaboration between policymakers and industry leaders.[19]

**

Chronic disease is highly prevalent in the US population, especially conditions like heart disease, cancer, and diabetes. Having a low income, living in a rural area, or being older are all risk factors that are highly associated with chronic illness. The people in these demographic categories also have comparatively lower access to the internet and smartphones than other groups, making the equitable delivery of digital healthcare models a challenge. But, the rates of smartphone ownership and internet access are increasing across all segments of the population.

Despite the disparities, looking at the current numbers, *more people than not* have a smartphone and internet access across any segment of the population. Thus, as these numbers continue to grow, the potential for the delivery of clinical services via smartphones is well established.

The problems of healthcare services and the health of the US population will not be solved through the simple fact that there is shift in modality from entirely face-to-face services to mixed virtual services. The improvement of access through the use of internet-delivered services is a crucial development in and of itself, but the real power of digitally enhanced care delivery allows for the creation of entirely new models of care and interventions to address health more holistically—and to measure performance in real time.

NOTES

1. Max Roser, Hannah Ritchie, and Esteban Ortiz-Ospina. "Internet." 2015. Published online at OurWorldInData.org. https://ourworldindata.org/internet [Online Resource]
2. Ibid.
3. Ibid.
4. Pew Research Center. "Mobile Technology and Home Broadband 2019." June 2019. Online. www.pewresearch.org
5. Ibid.
6. Ibid.
7. Ibid.
8. *National Healthcare Quality and Disparities Report Chartbook on Rural Health Care*. Rockville, MD: Agency for Healthcare Research and Quality; October 2017. AHRQ Pub. No. 17(18)-0001–2-EF.
9. Ibid.
10. Ibid.
11. Ibid.
12. Ibid.

13. Ibid.
14. This trend is driven by natural effects of aging but also can be impacted and exacerbated by lifestyle, socioeconomic factors, and access to healthcare services over time.
15. Pew Research Center. "Mobile Technology and Home Broadband 2019." June 2019. Online. www.pewresearch.org
16. Cambridge Dictionary, *s.v.* "Smartphone." Accessed August 2020. Online. https://dictionary.cambridge.org/us/.
17. This is a big current conversation and clear issue in the entirety of healthcare.
18. Pew Research Center. "Mobile Technology and Home Broadband 2019." June 2019. Online. www.pewresearch.org
19. The Covid-19 pandemic prompted a number of initiatives to address internet access and technology needs in rural areas and in impoverished populations. In the early days of the pandemic, the Federal Communications Commission launched a fund designed to extend this crucial access.

4

Refocusing Our Collective Efforts: Addressing Health Risk Factors

In reality, the major causes of chronic diseases are known, and if these risk factors were eliminated, at least 80% of all heart disease, stroke[,] and type 2 diabetes would be prevented; over 40% of cancer would be prevented.

—The World Health Organization

***

My mom had three distinct phases of her care journey spanning an eight-year timeframe beginning at her initial diagnosis. The first seven years were marked by a typical chronic care journey. She received care from her oncologist, in-person, at the outpatient clinic every three months. Thanks to some incredible advances on the biomedical side of healthcare innovation, tyrosine kinase inhibitors (TKIs), she was able to manage her chronic myeloid leukemia (CML) with two pills a day and visits with her oncologists at that three-month interval. For many years, she continued to teach fifth grade, run races, and live a relatively normal life.

This chronic care patient journey is very common and similar to the way patients with diabetes, hypertension, congestive heart failure (CHF), and other chronic illnesses receive care. Typically, patients receive in-person care every three to four months, with little interaction with a healthcare provider in the interim periods between in-person visits. Similarly, patients of higher risk may be seen every month, which is better but still leaves room for error. In this interim time, problems often arise.

The second phase of her journey was marked by a rapid deterioration and trip to the emergency room. The TKIs' efficacy waned after eight years, and her condition spiraled out of control. She was admitted to the hospital for several months as her condition worsened and she required chemotherapy to control the rapid growth of blood cells. While she was a patient with cancer, and the factors associated with the development of CML are unknown, many chronic illnesses can be managed in a manner that does not lead to a hospitalization.

She was under excellent care at the Bone Marrow Transplant Unit at Northside Hospital in Atlanta, Georgia. Nurses were available 24/7, and her condition was carefully monitored as we all navigated the situation. The cancer slowly came under control, but the treatment resulted in the development of CHF, a prolonged fungal blood infection, and significant weight loss. The third phase of her care was realized at discharge, or what is known as post-acute. Many patients are discharged to the home in the care of a family member, to the home with home health support, or to a post-acute care facility. But, too often, patients return to the hospital within a few weeks after their condition deteriorates once again. We returned a number of times after the initial discharge.

For my mom, the chronic care phase was marked by relative success. The goal of this period of care is for the patient to live a normal life of the highest quality. Many patients will go through the chronic phase, inpatient phase, and post-acute phase several times throughout their life. Each of these periods have their own risks. But the chronic phase and the post-acute phase represent periods with limited support or interaction with the health system, thus representing an opportunity to incorporate technology.

CHRONIC ILLNESS EPIDEMIOLOGY

Chronic disease does not have a unified definition—there is not a single taxonomy for the classification of chronic illness. Typically, chronic illnesses all share the element of lasting for a longer period of time than other conditions, and many are classified as a lifetime condition. Regardless, it is well known that these diseases contribute to a large proportion of global illnesses, with approximately one in three adults living with not just a single but multiple chronic conditions (MCC).[1]

Patients, like my mom, face a number of challenges when a single chronic illness is compounded with each additional diagnosis. Patients with MCC live with impacted quality of life, face potentially high expenses related to their care, experience limitations on ability to work, and feel additional impact on their mental health.[2]

The portion of healthcare expenditures directly attributable to chronic illness is important to note. Globally, healthcare expenditures attributed to chronic illness are high, and increasing, especially as the number of people experiencing MCC grows rapidly.[3] Expenses grow as patients require attention from multiple specialists and as emergency department visits and hospitalizations resulting from exacerbated conditions increase.

A 2017 report[4] by RAND Corporation, a major research nonprofit, analyzed the prevalence of chronic illness and the effect on US health-care spending. Figure 4.1 illustrates the high prevalence of chronic illness among US adults. Approximately 60% of US adults had at least one chronic condition.[5] This group of 60% of adults was linked to 90% of total healthcare spending. Twelve percent of US adults had more than five chronic conditions and were responsible for 41% of total healthcare spending. This group is considered to be the high-risk super spenders that are typically older and poorer than other populations.

In the US, the most impactful conditions with respect to prevalence in the country are outlined in Table 4.1.

Across the globe, and in the US, chronic illness prevention and management is the single most crucial area of health innovation due to the scale and cost of the problem. Rates of chronic illness in the US and in many regions have grown since 2000 despite advances in medical technology.[7] In the US, this is due, in part, to a failure of the healthcare delivery system to adequately implement models that effectively address the factors that

FIGURE 4.1
Chronic Illness and Multiple Chronic Illness in the US.[6]

TABLE 4.1

Prevalence of Chronic Illness Groups in the US

Condition	Prevalence
Hypertension	27%
Lipid disorders	21.6%
Mood disorders (e.g., depression, bipolar disorder)	11.9%
Diabetes mellitus	10.4%
Anxiety disorders	9.7%
Upper respiratory disorders	7.4%
Inflammatory joint disorders	7.4%
Osteoarthritis	6.5%
Asthma	6.3%
Coronary atherosclerosis	4.8%

Source: Buttorff, Christine, Teague Ruder, and Melissa Bauman, Multiple Chronic Conditions in the United States. Santa Monica, CA: RAND Corporation, 2017. www.rand.org/pubs/tools/TL221.html.

lead to and exacerbate chronic illness.[8] It is essential to invest not only in a wide range of societal interventions for this problem but also in the enhanced performance of existing health systems models of chronic disease care.

ADDRESSING FACTORS THAT LEAD TO CHRONIC DISEASE

The quote from the World Health Organization at the beginning of this chapter succinctly illustrates the need for more effective healthcare services and investment in public health systems. Many of the chronic illnesses that plague global populations are preventable. If not prevented, they are manageable and, sometimes, even reversible as with some cases of type 2 diabetes or hypertension.

The quote also references the reduction of *factors* that lead to the formation or exacerbation of chronic illness as the path to better chronic disease prevention and management. These factors are the drivers of chronic disease in populations.

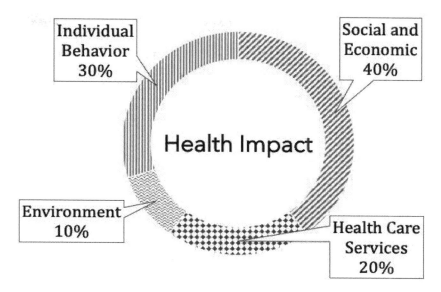

FIGURE 4.2
County Health Rankings Model of Factors Impacting Health.

In Figure 4.2, factors are grouped and summarized based on the County Health Rankings Model[9] produced by the University of Wisconsin Population Health Institute.

This model is one of several that outline the role of various factors that influence a person's health. While the percentages and categories differ slightly between the various models,[10] the overall themes that emerge are consistent. The primary take-away from each model is that healthcare services[11] have a comparatively smaller impact on health than individual behavior factors (e.g., lifestyle, diet, exercise), socioeconomic factors (e.g., racism-induced stresses, poverty, housing instability), and environmental factors (e.g., built environment, toxins, air pollution). It is particularly important to note that healthcare services, in their current form, only impact about 10% to 20% of healthcare outcomes. Holistically addressing all the factors experienced by the patient will be crucial to improving healthcare services and population health in societies around the globe.

Thus, I wish to offer the primary thesis for this book very explicitly: the injection of digital health technologies into healthcare services enables this relatively ineffective group of interventions to improve health by affecting factors that exist in the realm of individual behavior, socioeconomic, and environmental factors. This will not be achieved by the very act of injecting these technologies, but rather the programs that are built around them. At the same time, the introduction of technologies also improves the existing processes that reside firmly in the realm of traditional healthcare services. Said differently, digital health technologies allow us to rethink what we define as a healthcare service and to approach care for patients with chronic illness differently.

For example, under our current model, a healthcare provider might visit with a patient for 15 minutes to prescribe a medication. Under a new virtual care model, a 15-minute face-to-face visit might result in a prescription for medication as well as the assignment of a health coach who connects with the patient via an app to ensure that they know how to take their medications and are able to incorporate exercise into their daily life and educates on how to maintain a healthy diet in partnership with the patient. Rather than relying upon infrequent and time-resource-intensive face-to-face visits, this patient can instead connect with healthcare team members via an easy-to-use application. At the same time, this patient may also be screened via the app to identify depressive symptoms or socioeconomic factors that impact health outcomes. The patient can then receive a referral via the app to social services or mental health resources as needed. Thus, digital tools allow for continuous real-time connection between health experts and the patient while collecting important data related to the patient's health.

Many of the benefits associated with virtual care and technology-assisted healthcare services are derived from the expansion of traditional healthcare services into the areas of individual behavior and socioeconomic factors, while also streamlining and enhancing existing models of care and enabling the development of entirely new treatments and programs for patients. At the end of the day, innovation in chronic illness requires the relentless pursuit of *high-value services.*

*

When modern health policy leaders and reformists talk about value, value-based payment, and high-value services, they are often referring to the incentivization and subsequent provision of services that produce the "most health" for each dollar spent. Often these services fall into the category of preventive services. For example, one of the highest-value services that can be offered is a vaccination. Flu vaccinations, in particular, can help prevent a tremendous amount of disease, suffering, hospitalizations, and deaths for a relatively low price to prevented-cost ratio. Healthcare services that are high-value, like vaccinations, have a positive impact on health while preventing high-cost outcomes.

There is emerging work being done to better connect patients with high-value services outside of traditional healthcare services, but with positive effects on health. There is only so much the healthcare delivery system can offer due to a lack of societal investment in, control of, or coordination with social services. Thus, from a chronic disease perspective, there is potential for high-value socioeconomic interventions—coordinated by health services professionals. In my first book, *Innovating for Wellness*,[12] I discussed the use of digital tools[13] to allow for coordination of social services in this manner. For example, the provision of subsidized housing as well as the delivery of well-balanced meals to patients with type 2 diabetes are emerging as best practices. In a study by Berkowitz and colleagues,[14] patients with diabetes who were experiencing food insecurity received medically tailored meals. The program improved dietary quality and food security and reduced hypoglycemia. This type of intervention falls under the category of socioeconomic services, which, in this example, was delivered via a healthcare service organization. Technology can help facilitate the identification of patients in need, holistically allowing intervention into physiological, socioeconomic, behavioral, and environmental factors of disease, while assisting with efficient resource allocation.

Individual behavior risk factors are tough nuts to crack and have long been considered the holy grail of effective healthcare services, yet implementation at scale of effective and evidence-based models has been slow. Part of the reason for this is the significant time, staff requirements, and cost of programs that utilize health coaching, behavior education, and health counseling techniques. The availability of these clinicians and patient willingness to spend more time in a healthcare setting are major limiting factors, as is general medical acceptance of these models rather than a traditional prescription-writing mentality.

Indeed, a growing body of evidence from around the world suggests that, for multiple chronic conditions, health coaching and motivational interviewing techniques can produce positive health outcomes for patients. One randomized clinical study[15] in Taiwan suggests that a motivational interview–based program can improve patient self-management, hemoglobin A1C (HbA1C) control, self-efficacy, and quality of life over the standard of care.

Evidence also suggests that these high-touch models of care aimed at improving individual health behavior can sustain patient benefit beyond the program itself[16]—this means that they can offer benefit for a period of time after patients participate in the program. This perhaps leads to lifetime gains in health in the population and reduced cost to society. High-touch care models do, however, require significant time investment, and thus scalability has been hindered—this is where digital tools can lend a hand.

The factors that fall under the categories of individual behavior, environmental, and socioeconomic have long been the domain of public health, health policy, and health education—or thought to be solely the responsibility of the individual. Despite the evidence of their importance, medicine as an institution has focused heavily on the biomedical and physiological components of health. Medicine, as a field and profession, is the dominant driver of healthcare services. Thus, the provision of health services across the world is very focused on pathophysiological issues despite the evidence that other factors are far more impactful, or at least equally important. As far as clinical care delivery, traditional healthcare services have struggled to implement scalable high-touch models of care and interventions in collaboration with social services.

This issue is not new. In 1977, Dr. George Engel published his work[17] on the biopsychosocial model that suggests a multifactorial model of health rather than a strict biological one. Since that time, the field of medicine has not done well at including factors outside of the biological into practice. This is, in part, due to the challenges with implementation and the time required to meaningfully address other factors. When it comes down to the actual implementation of programs, prescribing a pill is relatively easy compared to spending time to perform a motivational interview and health coaching session with a patient or developing multi-stakeholder programs aimed at socioeconomic factors. Under the volume-driven FFS payment model in the US, where time is, quite literally, money, there is also a disincentive in the system for healthcare providers to spend more time with patients. In this case, the investment of time is necessary to drive positive health behavior change through motivational interviewing or health coaching programs.

This is one of the core issues, if not *the* core issue, in healthcare services today when it comes to improving the health of populations. The actual delivery of services does not reflect the experience of or address the factors associated with the patient's disease. This is like selling magazine printers to a digital-only publication or sending a plumber to fix an electrical problem. There is often an inherent mismatch between the needs of patients and the services offered by healthcare service organizations—and an inherent mismatch in the public's understanding that healthcare services, in their current form, do not produce as much positive impact on health as potentially other investments.

Digital health technologies help solve many of these implementation issues. From data collection that informs care personalization and patient risk factor identification, to communication functions that support program operations, to routing technologies that connect patients with the appropriate level of care team support, the use of mobile technology integrated into clinical programs has tremendous potential. The use of these technologies allows for high-touch models of care, that address a wider range of health factors, to be delivered at scale virtually rather than in a brick-and-mortar setting.

A NOD TO PUBLIC HEALTH AND SOCIAL INVESTMENT AT ALL LEVELS

While this book is about the use of digital health technologies for healthcare service purposes and does, in fact, primarily cover clinical care models for chronic disease, it is important to recognize an important truth. Medical and healthcare services alone are by no means the answer to our societal healthcare issues with chronic illness. They can certainly improve drastically and adopt a more holistic view of health. But, the most cost-effective and beneficial prevention measures must occur at the societal level.

The folks who work in public health proper will tell you that we must prioritize some major shifts from a societal level to truly improve population health—this is especially true in the US, where we lag behind many similar OECD nations that are further along in this area. In fact, if you read the public health literature, you will find that the majority of improvements we have seen in life expectancy and societal health metrics over the past 200 years have been due not to medical progress but to public health investment in areas like sanitation, health education, nutrition, and social services.

Social programs like low-income housing, low-income health coverage programs,[18] food access assistance, health education, fitness programs, and vaccinations are essential to improving the health of all people. Private and public investment in areas like homelessness, hunger, mental health services, lifestyle, worker's rights, and vaccination rates will likely yield better and more scalable results across populations than funneling investment into our healthcare service organizations. Indeed, in the US, the majority of our spend is on reactive health services rather than proactive ones.

But, as I see it, the emergence of digital health technologies can help in these areas as well. It takes a village to drive large-scale, societal impact. Together, through new technologies, governments and private organizations around the world can coordinate efforts to invest in and implement programs that focus on high-value services that raise the health of all people in a population.

Disease is inextricable from the existence of humanity. The reason we, as a society, should care about health is that a healthier society is more innovative, more productive and, morally, a worthy pursuit. In the end, a healthier and happier population should be the goal for countries across the globe. Healthier people have the ability to enjoy more quality time with their friends and family and navigate the experiences that make human existence unique.

NOTES

1. C. Hajat and E. Stein. "The Global Burden of Multiple Chronic Conditions: A Narrative Review." *Preventive Medicine Reports*, 12 (2018): 284–293. https://doi.org/10.1016/j.pmedr.2018.10.008
2. Ibid., 38.
3. Ibid.
4. Christine Buttorff, Teague Ruder, and Melissa Bauman. *Multiple Chronic Conditions in the United States*. Santa Monica, CA: RAND Corporation, 2017. Online. www.rand.org/pubs/tools/TL221.html.
5. Ibid.
6. Ibid., 40.

7. Ibid., 38.

8. The continued lack of investment in primary care services, universal health coverage mechanisms, and social services drives this trend in the US. In addition, the predominant payment model in the US, FFS, contributes heavily to performance issues in existing chronic disease care delivery.

9. County Health Rankings model, University of Wisconsin Population Health Institute, 2014.

10. Steven A. Schroeder. "We Can Do Better—Improving the Health of the American People." *New England Journal of Medicine,* 357(12) (2007): 1221–1228. https://doi.org/10.1056/NEJMsa073350.

11. Referring to services rendered under a traditional "medical model" rather than a holistic model of health. Healthcare services at their best, and when delivered holistically, can be effective.

12. Robert L. Longyear III. *Innovating for Wellness: Bridging the Gap between the Health System and Patient.* Washington, DC: New Degree Press, 2020.

13. See Unite Us.

14. S. A. Berkowitz, L. M. Delahanty, J. Terranova, et al. "Medically Tailored Meal Delivery for Diabetes Patients with Food Insecurity: A Randomized Cross-over Trial." *Journal of General Internal Medicine,* 34 (2019): 396–404. https://doi.org/10.1007/s11606-018-4716-z

15. Shu Ming Chen, Debra Creedy, Huey-Shyan Lin, and Judy Wollin. "Effects of Motivational Interviewing Intervention on Self-management, Psychological and Glycemic Outcomes in Type 2 Diabetes: A Randomized Controlled Trial." *International Journal of Nursing Studies,* 49(6) (2012): 637–644. ISSN 0020-7489. https://doi.org/10.1016/j.ijnurstu.2011.11.011

16. A. E. Sharma, R. Willard-Grace, D. Hessler, T. Bodenheimer, and D. H. Thom. "What Happens After Health Coaching? Observational Study 1 Year Following a Randomized Controlled Trial." *The Annals of Family Medicine,* 14(3) (2016): 200–207. https://doi.org/10.1370/afm.1924.

17. George L. Engel. "The Need for a New Medical Model: A Challenge for Biomedicine." (PDF). *Science,* 196(4286) (April 8, 1977): 129–136.

18. Especially for Primary Care.

5

Bridging and Adjusting
the Setting of Care

THE FACE-TO-FACE + VIRTUAL MODEL

"So be prepared, she is in a special unit with tight controls, you have to wear a gown, and there is a process to get into the sealed Bone Marrow Transplant floor," said my dad, as we walked from the parking garage during our trip, through the hospital hallways, up to my mom's floor—a route we would come to take hundreds of times.

She was admitted to the Bone Marrow Transplant (BMT) unit of Northside Hospital after difficulty breathing sent her to the emergency room. The BMT unit, as described by Northside Hospital, is the "inpatient home" for patients with blood cancer when hospitalization is indicated. Patients arrive at the BMT unit in various states of disease with some entering a new immediately life-threatening acute phase, some beginning the process of bone marrow transplant, and other patients receiving some other inpatient-delivered therapies.

As I approached the doors to the BMT unit at the end of a long hallway, I could see the "airlock" chamber that keeps the external environment out of the unit's sterile environment. This system is in place to minimize the risk of hospital-acquired infection. It is a hospital, so infection-causing microorganisms are everywhere, making the environment especially dangerous for immunocompromised patients with cancer.

We entered the airlock room, where we waited for the first set of doors to close before cleaning our bags, washing our hands, and donning protective gowns, shoe covers, masks, and hairnets. Once ready and clean, we hit the button to open the interior door of the unit.

Upon entering, I noticed that the hall was a racetrack-like setup. It was as if I had entered a flying saucer in some space film. Patient rooms flanked the perimeter, with the hallway wrapping around in a big interior set of rectangular rooms and counters. It was hard to believe that almost every one of the rooms was filled with a patient who was battling some stage of blood cancer.

In the center of the interior rectangle made by the hallway was the nurses' station, which was a low counter with desks behind it. There were family waiting rooms, conference rooms, and the snack room in the middle of the hallway.

We walked around the circle to my mom's room, which was located in a corner. I braced myself for the moment I would see her after two weeks of anticipation. We sanitized our hands as we opened the door and felt the rush of air pass when we released the positive pressure seal of the room.

I entered the dark room with my mom's hospital bed sitting directly in front of me. She was hooked up to at least seven IVs and corresponding IV pumps with bags of various colors hanging from the pole that was clearly designed to hold *many* bags.

As I walked into the room to greet my mom, I approached with caution and hesitation so as to not touch or move anything of importance. After moving on from the initial shock of the image, I moved past the mobile computer station that housed the hospital's Epic EMR. Like most modern hospital rooms, each patient room had a computer to allow for quick clinical data entry into the patients' medical records and the recording of the medical care provided—for billing purposes, of course.

My mom, who was still in pain from her swollen spleen driven by the excess of white blood cells in her body from the acceleration of her CML, was glad to see me but obviously anxious about her son seeing her in such a vulnerable and uncomfortable state.

After gaining a small but level amount of comfort in the room, we started to talk about how things were going. She had just started a five-day aggressive chemotherapy to reduce the cancer cells in her body and to, hopefully, bring her back into remission. It was clear to me that while she resembled herself, there was something less about her than the person she was outside the hospital.

In that room, we sat, uncertainty abounding. We were told that we could be there for 12 weeks or more, so we braced ourselves for the day-to-day life on the BMT unit, and, my mom, for her new 24/7 home. For an active, fifth grade–teaching, Tough Mudder–running, and generally social person, she had found her own personal hell full of discomfort, pain, loss of autonomy, nausea, and cabin fever—just like as many patients who find themselves admitted to the hospital for a lengthy stay. For this reason, I firmly believe that it is a worthy pursuit to search for means by which we can better prevent hospitalizations.

I spent most of my time observing processes as I paced around the floor hundreds of times. I paced and paced—sometimes for most of the night. Part of me wanted to see the way that healthcare was delivered day and night, and part of me, I now recognize, was unable to handle the emotional toll from the events unfolding before me and thus pacing and counting laps provided a small respite.

The monotonous environment took its toll on my mom. In that hospital room, she yearned for the relief of returning home as well as from her condition. The environment took its toll on all of us in her caregiver circle as we strove to funnel our own struggles into support for her. For weeks, we would ride the waves of positive and negative news, new symptoms, and the hope for discharge. During this time, while the acute cancer threat began to abate, her strength waned due to inactivity, lack of caloric intake, and the effects of the chemotherapy. Her original admission condition quickly became multiple new ones as the chemotherapy injured her heart and her compromised immune system struggled to defend against infection. This lead to intense daily uncertainty and a constant reminder of the precarious position she straddled between life and death.

Despite the challenges of hospitalization and her complex condition, her inpatient journey provided one benefit: she was monitored 24/7 by well-trained healthcare professionals. While discharge, in stable condition, was the goal, it represented a scary loss of access to round-the-clock medical knowledge, technologies, treatments, and monitoring.

Sending a patient home following a hospitalization is one of the most dangerous transitions across the continuum of healthcare. Inpatient services are intended to stabilize or monitor a high-severity or high-risk condition. Thus, afterward, there is often still recovery and rehabilitation required for patients. This period represents a precarious and potentially fragile time for patients. For us, it was no different.

These transitions of care are essential areas in which new technologies can improve patient outcomes and the cost associated with bad ones. In addition to post-acute transitions, patients receiving outpatient care for conditions experience impactful gaps in care between face-to-face appointments. Our health system is built on low-frequency, transactional, and face-to-face care that fails to adequately support patients in a way that reflects the longitudinal nature of their health. It reacts when it should prevent.

It is in post-acute transitions[1] and outpatient chronic care that digital technologies and virtual care models can bridge the gap between health services and the patient journey.

Post-Acute

My mom was discharged from her acute stay to our home. With a decent-sized group of family caregivers, she had round-the-clock care at home. However, the contrast between her care in the hospital and at home was stark for those of us who were tasked with monitoring her condition and caring for her. We prepared and managed it well as caregivers, but it was a monumental task. We were fortunate to have a good level of health literacy and some healthcare expertise—importantly, we knew when to ask for help. Unfortunately, many patients at home are not well supported or cared for by people who know when to ask for help.

My mom required four times daily vital sign monitoring, support eating, a long list of medications, and support with her activities of daily living (e.g., walking, dressing, and personal care). She was, perhaps, a candidate for a higher level of care post-discharge, but she was adamant about returning home after being confined to a hospital bed for months—so, we made it our mission to support her in this request.

When patients are discharged from the hospital, they are typically discharged to one of three places depending on their condition and perceived level of social support. The first location, for higher-risk patients, is the skilled nursing facility, where patients receive a hospital-like experience with skilled clinicians providing care. The second location is the home, with varying levels of home-health services where a nurse or other practitioner will visit the patient in the home to provide services. The third the home in the care of family members. Despite attempts at effective discharge planning in facilities, post-acute care transitions are still fraught with issues.

Post-acute care receives a large amount of attention from policymakers, physicians, and healthcare facilities. Patients are often in a stable but fragile health state at this point in their care journey. Frequently, this clinical state results in the higher likelihood of readmissions or deterioration that requires additional supportive care.[2] These readmissions are costly, and thus the attention is merited.

**

Readmissions after discharge from a hospital stay have been a major topic of discussion. In theory, if a hospital discharges a patient and that patient returns then the value of that original hospitalization is questionable. Reformers have suggested that the onus is on the healthcare facility to ensure adequate discharges that do not result in a readmission. While many readmissions of critically ill patients are unavoidable, research on the topic has shown that there are many likely preventable readmissions.

While this is a tricky area to classify, research suggests that approximately 15% of patients are readmitted to the hospital after discharge within 30 days.[3] Estimates of the proportion of those that are preventable vary widely, but the general consensus is that certain conditions[4] for which a hospitalization is originally initiated should not result in readmissions. Given this, policymakers have sought to address this issue. The Patient Protection and Affordable Care Act included provisions for the Hospital Readmission Reduction Program (HRRP) with the goal of reducing readmissions and bringing more attention to how healthcare organizations support patients after an acute discharge.[5]

The program began focusing on three conditions from which readmissions are most common and potentially preventable but has since grown to include the following conditions[6]: heart attacks, heart failure, pneumonia, chronic obstructive pulmonary disorder (COPD), hip and knee replacement, and coronary artery bypass graft procedures (CABG).

Critics of the program suggest that the treating hospital has limited ability to affect care after the patient leaves the facility—this is true. Incentives and disincentives built into the program sit at the hospital level, not on external providers, and the program itself does not inherently encourage collaboration in a manner that can actually reduce readmissions. Hospitals, thus, have explored a number of interventions and strategies to reduce readmissions.

Hospitals have explored low-tech and high-tech strategies. These range from clarifying patient discharge instructions and more robust discharge planning, improving care coordination efforts with post-acute care providers, communicating with patient primary care providers, and using both telehealth models and RPM.[7] Each of these strategies has the potential to be made more scalable and effective using digital technologies.

Due to the financial incentives and disincentives of the HRRP, hospitals have a large interest in solutions that can reduce readmissions. Thus, innovative health companies have been active in this area. In order to bridge the hospital–post-acute gap, virtual care programs have been developed to monitor patients remotely using wearables or medical devices to proactively identify patients at risk for readmission before it happens. The use of smartphones and mobile apps to better coordinate care between patients and a set of external providers is also a viable model. Beyond these more advanced, data-driven models, the use of audio-visual follow-up consultations between a discharging facility and the patient allows a hospital to reach patients when previously unable.

Outpatient Chronic Care: Driving Connected Care Models

In the first eight years after my mom's initial diagnosis, she received care in the outpatient setting, where her oncologist came to function as her primary care physician. Every three months, she would visit the clinic for blood work and a review of her condition. This model is consistent with the journey of most patients with chronic disease. Similarly, after a hospitalization, patients often receive care in the outpatient setting. Whether it is after an emergency department visit or hospitalization or after the initial diagnosis at an annual wellness visit, outpatient-driven care models are a major area of opportunity for digital health.

Outpatient care is the setting with which most people are familiar as it is the setting of most primary care practitioners (PCPs). Primary care is the health system's first line of defense once public health interventions, genetic processes, and individual behaviors fail or are refused. For many people without a diagnosis, the PCP experience is limited to an annual physical. For people with a chronic diagnosis, more frequent care occurs on a cycle based on the clinical complexity and number of conditions. When conditions exceed a certain threshold, PCPs often refer to specialists to provide additional input or expertise.

Effective primary care is essential. Studies show that countries with strong systems of primary care have better population health than those with less robust systems.[8] Additionally, many studies suggest that adequate access to primary care can lower overall healthcare utilization of a population[9,10,11,12] and can increase the use of preventive health services.[13] Patient care delivered through a primary care provider is also associated with more effective, cost-effective, and equitable health services.[14] Thus, from a strictly economic perspective,[15] it makes sense to ensure investment in this service line.

The United States lags behind other similar countries in primary care workforce and access to these essential services. In the US, the PCP workforce is roughly one-third of the entire physician workforce, which is a significantly smaller proportion than many similar OECD countries.[16] Part of the reason for this effect is the comparatively lower societal investment in primary care in the US than countries of a similar income level.[17]

This has major ramifications for the management of chronic disease in the US. While other countries are further along in primary care infrastructure investment and patient access, most are still driven by limited-duration face-to-face visits. Our models of chronic care are driven by brick-and-mortar locations that still present a major barrier to access and a poor ability of patients to engage with their health more frequently.

The typical patient with chronic illness might see a healthcare provider every three months or less frequently. One study[18] in the US found that patients have an average of 1.6 visits to a PCP[19] per year. In addition, one study looked at the average length of a primary care visit using 2015 data; it was 21.6 minutes.[20]

Referring back to the figure depicting the factors that impact health, 21.6 minutes is plenty of time to prescribe a medication and simply recommend to a patient that they exercise and improve their diet—it is not, however, enough time to adequately and holistically work with the patient to change lifestyle behaviors and to work to address social factors. Effective high-touch models of care require more engagement with and from patients. Without sufficient encouragement and opportunity to learn, a patient may only spend that same 21.6 minutes paying attention to their own health each year.

Thus, there is an opportunity for digital tools to extend the connection between a patient and their care team through the transmission of data and communication. A patient visit can go from 21.6 minutes of face-to-face interaction with a physician to continuous connection, access, and attention to health via a smartphone-based app. The ability to extend services and connection to a care team via a smartphone and into the daily life of the patient is a core benefit of digital health tools and virtual care models focused on chronic disease. Apps also present the ability to scale programs because many processes and requests can be automated and referred to a care team member as needed.

Brick-and-Mortar Barriers[21]

Healthcare services are currently inextricably linked to a brick-and-mortar location. The primary issue with tying health services to a physical location is the barriers it poses. In rural areas or countries with limited physical health infrastructure, healthcare services are unreachable by many people. Geographic access barriers to healthcare services or any needed social services are real issues. But, even in urban areas with a high density of healthcare providers, there are still barriers associated with brick and mortar.

A visit to a healthcare provider requires time. For many people, time is money. If the choice is to take time off from work to attend a clinic visit or to make rent that month—rent is going to take precedence. This is an inherent flaw in a physical location–based healthcare delivery system. Socioeconomic inequities are important to recognize in order to address them. This type of barrier is experienced disproportionately by populations of low-income and people of color. Making health services more accessible is an act that can work toward health equity.

If the time is money effect is not as strong for certain groups, a trip to the clinic is still a decision point. Time is a valuable resource. Would you rather spend time with your loved ones watching Hallmark movies or would you rather drive to the clinic in traffic in order to sit in an outpatient waiting room for 45 minutes to see a healthcare provider for 21.6 minutes? While many will choose to prioritize their health, there will be many who do not.

Making health services more effective at managing chronic illness requires making them accessible for all people: not just accessible but so seamless that they incorporate nicely into daily life and so that taking care of one's health is as easy as picking up a smartphone.

**

For those fiscally responsible for the healthcare spending of a population, preventing readmissions or admissions in the first place makes good moral and economic sense. Hospitalizations are expensive. In fact, research done by the Agency for Healthcare Research and Quality (AHRQ) using the National Health Expenditure Data shows that hospital care is responsible for $0.39 of every dollar spent on healthcare services, or 39% of spending.[22]

Just like preventable readmissions after a previous discharge, unplanned and preventable hospitalizations are most frequently proceeded by an emergency department visit or scheduled outpatient clinic appointment that results in abnormal findings. The goal of many healthcare innovation initiatives is to reduce emergency department visits and inpatient utilization. The improvement of primary care services in order to prevent and stabilize patients' chronic illnesses is one way of accomplishing this goal.

Many hospitalizations are preventable. AHRQ defines these episodes of care as:

> Potentially preventable hospitalizations are admissions to a hospital for certain acute illnesses (e.g., dehydration) or worsening chronic conditions (e.g., diabetes) that might not have required hospitalization had these conditions been managed successfully by primary care providers in outpatient settings.

The key word in that definition is part about successfully managing chronic conditions in the primary care setting. Currently, our models of chronic disease care are insufficient. Too often patients are hospitalized, or require more intensive care services, due to a deteriorating, but medically-manageable, chronic illness like diabetes. In the time outside of the clinic, patients' experiences with health are highly varied. Poor health behaviors, socioeconomic risk factors, improper care coordination, and poor self-management can quickly lead to a hospitalization.

Once a patient's condition has deteriorated far enough to merit hospitalization, the goal often becomes keeping the patient alive and getting an out-of-control physiological process back into a normal range. Thus, the time spent in the hospital is still spent on managing the "sick" condition and not on preventing the same occurrence from happening again.

This cycle of chronic disease stabilization and lack of sustained support from the health system is one of the major areas in which digital health tools will impact healthcare around the world. The ability to connect with patients in real time, to collect clinical data, and to provide a supportive hand should not be overlooked and will drive major changes to how healthcare is delivered over the next 30 years.

**

The role of virtual care in the post-acute and daily chronic care spaces is still evolving. With ubiquitous smartphones that can collect data, enable communication with a wide spectrum of healthcare professionals, and deliver educational content, the potential for the creation of effective interventions is high.

Many patients in the post-acute space will always need in-person care to help with activities of daily living and other medical services. However, the ability to deliver additional expertise to the patient home, efficiently, is a powerful tool. Patient check-ins, virtually, can be quick and can reveal potential risk factors and deterioration prior to a costly readmission.

In practice, solutions that enable connected care models through the use of digital technologies have shown positive benefit in the prevention of readmissions and health outcomes. One study[23] of patients with CHF discharged to a skilled nursing facility and to the home shows us that virtual care models can be effective. Wireless sensors were provided to patients to be worn in order to capture clinical metrics related to CHF care. Depending on the data, patients had both scheduled and data-driven video visits with a heart failure clinician. The patients who received this intervention had a 29% lower hospital readmission rate despite the fact that these patients had a much higher predicted risk of readmission. As secondary outcomes from this study, patients reported high satisfaction and improvements to their self-care knowledge for their condition.

Digital technologies shift the setting of care from episodic and in-person to continuous and flexible. Meeting patients where they are is an essential principle that underlies the implementation of digital health-based clinical models. When this is accomplished, patients become more engaged in a way that fits their life outside of the clinic. In the current, in-person paradigm, health services become an errand or a line item on a list of competing priorities. In a digital-enabled service model, patients can participate in their health in a way that does not compete with other activities, while healthcare organizations can develop new, more flexible, and scalable models of care that prioritize high-value services.

NOTES

1. I'll lump post-operative transitions in here, too.
2. E. E. Vasilevskis, J. G. Ouslander, A. S. Mixon, S. P. Bell, J. M. Jacobsen, A. A. Saraf, . . . J. F. Schnelle. "Potentially Avoidable Readmissions of Patients Discharged to Post-Acute Care: Perspectives of Hospital and Skilled Nursing Facility Staff." *Journal of the American Geriatrics Society*, 65(2) (2016): 269–276. https://doi.org/10.1111/jgs.14557
3. T. Braes, P. Moons, P. Lipkens, et al. "Screening for Risk of Unplanned Readmission in Older Patients Admitted to Hospital: Predictive Accuracy of Three Instruments." *Aging Clinical and Experimental Research*, 22(4) (2010): 345–351. https://doi.org/10.1007/BF03324938
4. According to the Centers for Medicare and Medicaid Services: acute myocardial infarction, COPD, heart failure, pneumonia, CABG surgery, and elective primary total hip arthroplasty and/or total knee arthroplasty.
5. N. R. Desai, J. S. Ross, J. Y. Kwon, et al. "Association Between Hospital Penalty Status Under the Hospital Readmission Reduction Program and Readmission Rates for Target and Nontarget Conditions." *JAMA*, 316(24) (2016): 2647–2656. https://doi.org/10.1001/jama.2016.18533
6. These conditions are all common and result from a failure to prevent their development. Our lack of focus on the factors that lead to chronic disease has driven the high prevalence in many developed countries, but especially in the US.
7. F. S. Ahmad, et al. "Identifying Hospital Organizational Strategies to Reduce Readmissions." *American Journal of Medical Quality*, 28(4) (2013): 278–285; S. Silow-Carroll, et al. *Reducing Hospital Readmissions: Lessons from Top-Performing Hospitals*. Commonwealth Fund Synthesis Report. New York: Commonwealth Fund, 2011; B. W. Jack, et al. "A Reengineered Hospital Discharge Program to Decrease Hospitalization: A Randomized Trial." *Annals of Internal Medicine*, 50(3) (2009): 178–187; S. B. Kanaan. *Homeward Bound: Nine Patient-Centered Programs Cut Readmissions*. Oakland, CA: California HealthCare Foundation, 2009.
8. J. Macinko, B. Starfield, and L. Shi. "The Contribution of Primary Care Systems to Health Outcomes within Organization for Economic Cooperation and Development (OECD) Countries, 1970–1998." *Health Services Research*, 38(3) (2003): 831–865.
9. S. Greenfield, E. C. Nelson, M. Zubkoff, et al. "Variations in Resource Utilization among Medical Specialties and Systems of Care. Results from the Medical Outcomes Study." *JAMA*, 267(12) (1992): 1624–1630.
10. C. B. Forrest and B. Starfield. "The Effect of First-contact Care with Primary Care Clinicians on Ambulatory Health Care Expenditures." *Journal of Family Practice*, 43(1) (1996): 40–48.
11. J. P. Bynum, A. Andrews, S. Sharp, D. McCollough, and J. E. Wennberg. "Fewer Hospitalizations Result When Primary Care is Highly Integrated into a Continuing Care Retirement Community." *Health Affairs (Millwood)*, 30(5) (2011): 975–984.
12. J. O. Tom, C. W. Tseng, J. Davis, C. Solomon, C. Zhou, R. Mangione-Smith. "Missed Well-child Care Visits, Low Continuity of Care, and Risk of Ambulatory Care-sensitive Hospitalizations in Young Children." *Archives of Pediatrics and Adolescent Medicine*, 164(11) (2010): 1052–1058.

13. A. B. Bindman, K. Grumbach, D. Osmond, K. Vranizan, A. L. Stewart. "Primary Care and Receipt of Preventive Services." *Journal of General Internal Medicine,* 11(5) (1996): 269–276.

14. B. Starfield. "Refocusing the System." *The New England Journal of Medicine,* 359(20) (2008): 2087–2091

15. I think it is also the right thing to do.

16. American Medical Association (AMA). "AMA Physician Masterfile." Accessed January 2, 2018. Online. www.ama-assn.org/life-career/ ama-physician-masterfile.

17. Patient-Centered Primary Care Collaborative, Robert Graham Center. "Investing in Primary Care: A State-Level Analysis." 2019. Web. https://www.pcpcc.org/ resource/investing-primary-care-state-level-analysis

18. S. M. Petterson, W. R. Liaw, R. L. Phillips Jr, D. L. Rabin, D. S. Meyers, and A. W. Bazemore. "Projecting US Primary Care Physician Workforce Needs: 2010–2025." *Annals of Family Medicine,* 10(6) (2012, November–December): 503–509.

19. Defined as a general practitioner, family physician, pediatrician, geriatrician, or general internist. Also, this estimate varies widely depending on methodology, so this study should be viewed in that regard.

20. Aarti Rao, et al. "National Trends in Primary Care Visit Use and Practice Capabilities, 2008–2015." *The Annals of Family Medicine,* 17(6) (2019): 538–544. https://doi.org/10.1370/afm.2474.

21. I thought this was exceptionally catchy, so I made this footnote. Got to squeeze in some personality here and there.

22. Agency for Healthcare Research and Quality, Healthcare Cost and Utilization Project, State Inpatient Databases disparities analytic file, 2009.

23. A. Dadosky, H. Overbeck, L. Barbetta, K. Bertke, M. Corl, K. Daly, . . . S. Menon. "Telemanagement of Heart Failure Patients Across the Post-Acute Care Continuum." *Telemedicine and E-Health,* 24(5) (2018): 360–366. https://doi. org/10.1089/tmj.2017.0058

6

Telemedicine: The Genesis of Virtual Care

Dr. Richard Boxer left his urology residency with a passion for political science and the careful skills of a surgeon. His interest in politics would quickly lead him to pursue opportunities in health policy with the Gore Campaign in the 1980s.

"I decided to look for a potential candidate for the presidency, get to know that person[,] and understand how that whole process works," described Dr. Boxer.

Richard got involved writing health policy for Gore and leading campaign events in the pivotal state of Wisconsin during his first campaign. "Unfortunately," explained Boxer, "Gore lost to Dukakis, but I continued to become closer with him, his family, and staff. Several of us were encouraging him to run in 1992, while he was writing a book called *Earth in the Balance*. Unfortunately, his son was hit by a car, and, with him constantly at his son's bedside, he knew he could not make another run in 1992. He encouraged us to seek another candidate." Dr. Boxer began to search for his next political outlet. It was not until a young governor from Arkansas entered the national scene that he identified his next opportunity.

"I got to know Bill and Hillary and their staff. I was doing surrogate speaking and writing health policy for him during the campaign. When Clinton was elected, I was put on the transition committee for healthcare."

Boxer got very involved in the health policies under the Clinton Administration. In 1996, he was asked by President Clinton to be his senior advisor for health policy in his campaign. In 1997, Dr. Boxer was a finalist for Surgeon General of the United States; although he was passed over for the position, he remained involved in the administration.

At this point in the conversation during our interview, I was wondering how all this was going to relate to health technology and telemedicine—it sounded a lot like health policy.

"I know this is all ancient history, but it is all related to how I got involved at the beginning of telemedicine," Boxer added, "what happened next in telemedicine was very influential. George W. Bush appointed Tommy Thompson to be secretary of HHS and, at the time, I had a good relationship with Tommy—we were both from Wisconsin."

Thompson, now US Secretary of Health and Human Services, told Dr. Boxer that he wanted to reach across the aisle to appoint him as Surgeon General. With Boxer, a Democrat, and Thompson, a Republican—it was a rare show of bipartisanship. After interviews with senators, the appointment went all the way to the West Wing. At this point, Karl Rove, then Deputy Chief of Staff, instantly rejected the idea of having a Democrat in the Administration."

"Always the bridesmaid, never the bride," joked Boxer during our conversation.

So, Dr. Boxer, Surgeon General candidate, accomplished urologist, and health policy advisor, was back in Wisconsin. But, what turned out happening was only possible due to his preceding rejection from the Surgeon General role.

"In a couple of years, Thompson left as the Secretary of HHS. Tommy was offered a tsunami of opportunities, one of which was from a nearly bankrupt company, Teladoc, to be on the Board of Directors. But, he said he would only join if Richard Boxer was Chief Medical Officer," Dr. Boxer explained.

So, he evaluated the opportunity to join Teladoc and eventually decided to take the plunge into the true genesis of the telemedicine industry during the summer of 2006.

"At the beginning, I was asking myself what doctor in their right mind would do something like this," said Boxer. After some internal debate, however, he recognized that his entire policy career in the public sector was trying to provide access to affordable and convenient quality care. In the private sector, the answer, to Boxer, was telemedicine.

At the time Dr. Boxer joined Teladoc, there were three major players in the telemedicine space. American Well, now AmWell, and MDLive, were the other two competitors. Telemedicine was still in the early days where physicians would sign up, go through training, and provide limited primary care services to patients.

At this point, telemedicine provided important access to healthcare services for patients who may not have geographic proximity to clinics. The industry really, truly was just telemedicine. It was physician-driven medical services provided through a technology platform where a patient and physician were matched together for a conversation via audio and video transmission.

Since that time, telemedicine has undergone some important evolution. But the concept of telemedicine proper, that is the physician–patient video connection, has not deviated far from that format. Whether it is a patient accessing a technology in the home or a specialist consultation from facility to facility, telemedicine is a physician practicing medicine from a distance through an audio/video technology or asynchronously.

But in the years since the big three telemedicine companies entered the scene, there has been a rapid expansion of what it means to deliver healthcare services. New healthcare providers, levels of clinician, and specialties have become increasingly important. And, technology has advanced beyond simple audio-visual capabilities.

SCOPE OF CARE

The Federation of State Medical Boards defines[1] scope of practice as "the activities that an individual healthcare practitioner is permitted to perform within a specific profession. Those activities should be based on appropriate education, training, and experience."

An expanded definition may include the location or the setting of care as a factor when determining the activities an individual healthcare provider should be legally permitted to provide. In telemedicine, or virtual care, broadly, scope of practice is an important topic.

"I had to produce and create all the documents, policies, and procedures. It became the standard around the country. It was really different. At the time, we were considered rogue doctors," explained Dr. Boxer, "going from rogue to mainstream in 12 years was absolutely light speed for medicine in general. Keep in mind it took 16 years for doctors to accept the stethoscope."

At the time Dr. Boxer began, telemedicine was very novel. The digital revolution had not yet taken hold in 2006 when Teladoc was just starting. Keep in mind, the iPhone was not released until mid-2007. Physicians and regulators were skeptical and the largest source of criticism was *scope of practice.*

"People would say as a reason not to do telemedicine: how can you help a patient when you don't have the patient in the same room as you," recalled Boxer. "I would tell them that doctors are taught in medical school that 80% of diagnoses are determined by the patient's history. Further, I would ask the highly resistant regulatory boards what the term was when a doctor cared for a colleague's patient when the doctor was not available: the phrase is 'being on call.'"

Dr. Boxer's campaign to gain adoption among the state regulatory boards was effective and based firmly in the idea that physicians both are capable of providing certain services via telemedicine and were already operating in a health system where telephonic consultations and interactions were common.

Nonetheless, the criticism had, and still has, some legitimacy in that the proportion of medical services that can delivered via a standard telemedicine platform are limited to low-risk, acute care. Dr. Boxer conceded that Teladoc's services were limited in terms of scope. Scope of care without consideration of chronic illness must be carefully considered and indeed should be the purview of clinicians who know the patient and their health over time. For conditions that require lifetime management, a clinical relationship is essential to ensure quality care for a patient.

For the past 20 years or so of telemedicine, the majority of visits have been follow-ups to in-person care services or 15-minute calls with a physician for a non–life-threatening, urgent (defined by the patient) illnesses such as upper respiratory or urinary tract infections. While this is a bit hyperbolic, the concept is true—scope of practice is truly limited in comparison to face-to-face services given the medical resources available in many healthcare facilities and the current emphasis on biomedical tests and medical device diagnostics.

The scope of practice when a physician is not able to run tests, touch the patient, or utilize medical devices is somewhat limited and the physician time available to allocate to patient care is still too short over telemedicine, where reimbursement has been historically lower than in-person services.

Despite scope issues, Dr. Boxer estimates that at least 25% of the 1.2 billion medical consultations that occur in the US each year can be effectively handled by telemedicine, and without a risk of lower quality.

Dr. Boxer emphasized that while scope of practice is a present challenge with traditional telemedicine, the improved access to care resulting from telemedicine services is something of great value. In the United States, the improved delivery of specialists from facility to facility and the provision of care to rural areas are two of the major successes of telemedicine programs.

In global health, the ability to deliver medical expertise to remote areas around the globe has been greatly enhanced by telemedicine. Global health professionals operating around the world can now reach patients wherever the Internet can take them. Local hospitals around the world without onsite neurologists, psychiatrists, or other specialists can now access this expertise via the power of telemedicine services.

I asked Dr. Boxer what he was most excited about in the journey and what he sees as the future for telemedicine.

"I am proud that I helped create an industry that improves access to care and changed the paradigm of healthcare delivery. This is about affordable access to quality care for patients," Boxer stated, "the future of this space is in chronic illness and expanding the scope of care for the services offered remotely. Chronic care is where the greatest amount of money is expended and can be accomplished with monitors and wearables to bring vital signs and other data to the provider. I see no scenario in the future of health care that does not include virtual care as a more complete version expanding from traditional telemedicine."

TELEMEDICINE PAYMENT POLICY

I would be remiss if I did not mention the single largest driver of telemedicine adoption by physicians—payment policy. In an effort to curb potentially high utilization due to the convenience, telemedicine reimbursement has historically been lower than in-person services. Lower reimbursement may also reflect a belief that telemedicine services are less effective than face-to-face services.

Commercial payors have limited their reimbursement to preferred tele-medicine partners and have followed the lead of Medicare in reimbursing telemedicine visits at a lower rate than in-person services. Medicaid programs have been limited in their scope of telemedicine reimbursement, with large variation across each state program. States like Georgia, at one point, mandated that telemedicine services must be rendered at a physical location where satellite offices staffed by medical assistants would provide telemedicine access to physicians located in a remote location.

The reason for lower reimbursement is largely to curb overutilization by patients. The barrier to access telemedicine is lower than in-person services, and thus the fear has been unnecessary utilization of the care modality. Telemedicine's most important feature, access, has also been a potential driver of lower reimbursement.

CMS has maintained policies that limit the utilization of telemedicine services for years until the 2020 Covid-19 pandemic. When Covid-19 hit, telemedicine services received payment parity with in-person services because of the risk of viral infection resulting from in-person office visits.

**

In the healthcare services community, there is little opposition to the idea that a video conference with a physician is convenient, is effective for some appointment types, and has a major place in the future of the industry. The primary points of contention that impact adoption are driven by discomfort with change and lack of consistent payment parity between in-person and telemedicine visits.

In 2018, a study[2] by Carol Kane and Kurt Gillis of the American Medical Association looked at physician adoption and use of telemedicine services. Looking at 2016 nationally representative survey data, they found that 15.4% of physicians reported working at facilities that used telemedicine in some form. The same survey showed that 11.2% of physicians worked in organizations using telemedicine for interactions between physicians and other healthcare professionals (e.g., facility to facility).

The research also found that larger practices or organizations were more likely to utilize telemedicine in either form likely due to larger budgets and ability to operationalize. This finding supports the idea that financial reasons are the largest barrier to adoption of telemedicine services.

Besides payment as a barrier to adoption, the institutional inertia of medicine also contributes to a slow adoption rate. Medicine as an institution has operated in much the same format for thousands of years. In our recent medical history, say around the early 1900s, physicians still made house calls and were very limited in their ability to diagnose, treat, and assist patients in managing conditions—especially compared to today.

Physician training is still centered around in-person care, and virtual care models are not prioritized in medical education. The evidence,[3] however, suggests that the single largest barrier to the adoption of telehealth services is still the cost of the technology and the lack of payment coverage despite the cultural headwinds.

Dr. Boxer's take on the future of telemedicine is the expansion of the scope of practice to chronic disease health services through the merging and crossing-over of technologies and terminologies. No longer is telemedicine just a physician video or telephonic conferencing with a patient. The digital health world is expanding rapidly as shown by the addition of new terms like virtual care, RPM, connected care, and telehealth. These terms, as mentioned before, are starting to dominate the healthcare landscape.

New clinicians are also being added to the equation as nurses, nurse practitioners, psychologists, health coaches, medical assistants, pharmacists, and other clinicians are being added to the mix of virtual care teams. No longer are visits just between a physician and patient. The world of virtual care models is expanding to develop entirely new models of care delivery.

Home-based lab tests are being shipped to patients to provide clinical insights to remote providers. RPM and the addition of wearable medical devices bring the power of patient-generated data collection to traditional telemedicine combined with the collaboration with more clinical specialties. This trend will allow the scope of practice to expand into chronic conditions.

NOTES

1. Federation of State Medical Boards. Assessing Scope of Practice in Health Care Delivery: Critical Questions in Assuring Public Access and Safety Adopted as policy by the Federation of State Medical Boards in 2005.
2. C. K. Kane and K. Gillis. "The Use of Telemedicine By Physicians: Still The Exception Rather Than The Rule." *Health Affairs*, 37(12) (2018): 1923–1930. https://doi.org/10.1377/hlthaff.2018.05077
3. Ibid.

7

Telemedicine: The Evidence

Dr. Boxer's experience with the state regulatory boards is a good example of one of the great mysteries of telemedicine and an example of the significant institutional inertia that exists in medicine and healthcare services in general. It is also a testament to the persistence of an individual to change the delivery of healthcare in order to vastly improve access to convenient and affordable care without the loss of quality.

The mystery, to me, is why the concept of audio-visual telemedicine is so difficult to grasp by many individuals. Dr. Boxer spent a good deal of time and effort convincing people that this is something that should be done to improve access, could be done safely, and was essentially already done currently. He reminded me that the first telemedicine consult was by Alexander Graham Bell when he first called Dr. Watson 150 years ago.

Regardless of the specific mix of drivers surrounding telemedicine adoption hesitancy, there is still some degree of mystery in why the concept of audio-visual telemedicine is so novel to many people. Growing up during the years that bridge pre– and post–digital revolution may shape my thinking about this, but communicating with patients remotely using audio/video technologies does not seem like much of an innovation at all—it seems like a natural development.

During my mom's care after her hospital discharge, we spent hours in the car each week driving back and forth between the outpatient clinic and our home in suburban Atlanta. While lab tests were an essential part of her care and telemedicine video consults would not have been possible at every visit, there were a number of occasions where information and check-ins could have been performed via telemedicine. At this point in her care journey, my mom had lost 30 pounds and was unable to walk on her own, and the trip to and from the clinic was physically and emotionally taxing. We made the 45-minute trips to the clinic and often sat around waiting for information to be delivered—many of these circumstances called for telemedicine out of respect for patient comfort.

Similarly, at a particularly dire point in her care journey, the decision was made to seek a second opinion from the longtime Leukemia Department head at MD Anderson Cancer Center at the University of Texas. Widely considered to be one of the top cancer centers in the world, this trip was a bit of a "Hail Mary of Hope" for a new treatment option as the current standards of care began to show waning efficacy. It was a two-day trip by car to reduce the risk of infection from air travel. In the end, the visit was a review of her existing medical records for 30 minutes. The outcome was a new treatment recommendation to be administered by her existing physician in Atlanta—something that was exceptionally disappointing and that could have been performed via facility-to-facility telemedicine—this outcome is something that was likely driven by payment differences between in-person and telemedicine visits at the expense of patient experience and comfort.

It is important to recognize the various forms of physician-driven audio-visual telemedicine. Most often discussed, and the focus of this book, is the direct-to-consumer model where a physician has a visit directly with a patient. Companies like Teladoc provide direct-to-patient telemedicine access via an online portal. In this case, Teladoc operates like a national medical practice that only delivers care via audio-visual modalities.[1]

The second form is the use of direct-to-patient telemedicine by a physician practice with an existing relationship. A local physician practice or other healthcare facility under this mode may offer telemedicine as a distinct service line or for patient follow-ups. In this case, the longitudinal patient relationship may not be too much of an issue if telemedicine visits are used between a physician with an existing longitudinal relationship.

The third form is facility-to-facility, or physician-to-facility, which is most often the provision of remote specialists into an area with a dearth of medical expertise. This could be emergency physicians using telemedicine to supplement a rural emergency department with only primary care physicians on staff. This could be a neurocritical care specialist using telemedicine to ensure adequate stroke care in facilities without access to a sufficient number of physicians in this subspecialty. Other examples are acute psychiatric care and acute cardiac events that may require advanced drugs or specialized expertise. Thus, patients are cared for in person by a healthcare professional who is advised by a remote clinician with specialized expertise.

These three models provide expanded patient access to care and convenience for patients. Regardless of the form telemedicine takes, many critics of telemedicine cite concerns about quality of care, cost-effectiveness, and patient satisfaction—all of which are barriers to adoption and the inclusion of digital technologies as tools in evolving chronic care clinical models.

**

In healthcare, there are a number of variables at play when evaluating new innovations, technologies, treatments, or clinical models. Does it cost more or less? Does it provide benefit to the patient in terms of improving their condition? Does it improve the patient's experience? Does it save time? Does it prioritize a patient's comfort and quality of life? Does it improve access to care without loss of quality? Of particular interest during the Covid-19 pandemic of 2020, does it prevent infection risk to the healthcare worker and/or the patient?

These questions are important to answer in a highly regulated industry that relies on complex systems, a multispecialty workforce, and tight cost control at all levels. At the top of mind in most circumstances (well-placed cynicism aside) is the question: does this new innovation provide benefits to patient health outcomes? The goal of health services, after all, is to improve the health of the population.[2] In Dr. Boxer's words, "This is a merger, at long last, of individual healthcare and public health."

When we ask ourselves these questions about traditional telemedicine between a physician and a patient, the addition of audio/visual technology does not seem to fundamentally alter the core of the interaction. Outside of the scope of practice issue, for services that are reasonably able to be performed via audio/visual telemedicine, the interaction between physician and patient is largely the same as an in-person consultation, with the important exception of the ability to perform a physical examination.[3]

A physician, and their body of knowledge, meets the patient with their experience of the present illness. A first-time consultation might bring a review of the patient's symptoms, a discussion of medical history, and the provision of a diagnosis and treatment plan. With a limited scope of practice, this might be the diagnosis of a sinus or a skin infection. Or, given an established relationship, the physician may perform a check-in with the patient given an existing body of knowledge of both the principles of medicine and the patient's medical history. The outcome from this visit might involve the titration of an already prescribed medication. Should both of these hypothetical visits occur in person, it is likely that the interaction and results would follow a similar form.

Individually, this conceptually makes sense. But, in healthcare services and policy, the next layer of concern becomes what happens at the population level when a particular modality meets hundreds, then thousands, then millions of individuals. Reviewing the large-scale evidence for telemedicine across larger patient populations and a wide range of specialties, conditions, and interventions is essential to understanding its place in healthcare moving forward. What variables does telemedicine improve at the population level? Does it extend access to those without it? Does the improvement of access lead to gains in population health? Does it improve or deliver comparable quality of care to face-to-face services? Does it increase patient satisfaction? Does it improve patient safety?

TELEMEDICINE: THE EVIDENCE

A PubMed search for the term "telemedicine" yields about 36,000 research article results. The first articles seem to appear in 1974 and begin to grow in number rapidly around the mid-1990s. By the 2010s, there were thousands of articles published annually that fall under the "telemedicine" search term.

The question at hand is: what do we know about traditional telemedicine as it compares to in-person services?

A rapid review of the evidence for telehealth,[4] performed by Erin Shigekawa and colleagues in 2018, provides some insight into the effectiveness of telemedicine as it relates to health outcomes. Based on this evidence, it is likely that telemedicine is broadly comparable to in-person services on an individual basis, but it could have societal benefit to population health should the access improvements lead to meaningful benefit over time.

To assess the current state of the evidence for differences between in-person care and telehealth services, the researchers evaluated published clinical studies on the topic. To perform their review, they searched databases of research publications for systematic reviews and meta-analyses that cover the use of telehealth services by patients of any age and for any condition published between January 2004 and May 2018.

The individual *systematic reviews* are studies that review hundreds of additional individual clinical studies that evaluate telehealth compared to in-person services. Essentially, this research,[5] published in *Health Affairs*, looks at all the available empirical information on telehealth versus in-person care and attempts to synthesize it. This study included 20 systematic review articles that cover a wide mix of specialties and points of care along the healthcare continuum.

The specific interventions included[6] were any diagnosis or treatment delivered via live videoconferencing; asynchronous store and forward of data; or telephone, email, text, or chat messaging directly with a healthcare provider. This review does not necessarily cover RPM, though many of the studies could have this as a component.

The comparison groups in this review were telehealth versus in-person care services. The goal of the rapid review study was to assess potential differences in outcomes between telehealth services and in-person services. Specific outcomes evaluated include health outcomes (e.g., change in symptoms or condition metrics), process outcomes (e.g., diagnostic accuracy), and utilization outcomes (e.g., inpatient utilization, emergency department visits, and outpatient service utilization).

When it comes to telemedicine in general, the goal of the outcome is equivalence with in-person usual care and, importantly, this study suggests that the two modalities are essentially equivalent. The authors conclude with the following statement:

> Broadly, telehealth interventions appear generally equivalent to in-person care.

However, this study suggests that telehealth's impact on the use of other services is unclear. One of the burning questions in the field is currently: what is the correct mix of services between in-person care and care delivered virtually?

Despite some current unknowns, the primary benefit of telehealth, or telemedicine, is widely accepted and acknowledged to be enhanced access to care for patients with geographic or other barriers to in-person clinical services as well as improvements in patient experience.

Outside of quality of care, it is also essential that new innovations pass the test of cost-effectiveness. Does telemedicine lead to more frequent emergency department visits? Does it reduce them? Does it lead to more in-person services? Does a full-scale telemedicine program cost more than the current in-person clinic set-up?

COST CONSIDERATIONS

I performed an additional review of the literature to better understand the potential cost implications of telemedicine services. I ran into three major problems. These three issues with the literature are common across research questions related to clinical effectiveness, cost-effectiveness, and patient satisfaction, but they are especially clear in cost-effectiveness evaluations in telemedicine.

The first issue was the same definitional problem where systematic reviews were evaluating programs that are not necessarily comparable. Some programs utilized RPM plus video conferencing technology. Some programs were telemedicine proper. Some programs were RPM alone. At a basic level, this major definitional issue causes a problem for determining the efficacy and cost-effectiveness of interventions delivered via digital technologies. It also causes major issues for implementation and the scalability of programs as decision-makers in healthcare organizations have many different understandings of models of care classified under telehealth or telemedicine—or, any of the other terms.

The second issue that arose in many of the systematic reviews is the methods by which researchers evaluated cost-effectiveness. Given the cost of the actual telemedicine intervention itself, additional patient costs associated with their conditions, and the use of healthcare resources over time, there is much variation in the methods used to compare cost-effectiveness of telemedicine versus in-person standards of care.

The third issue is that many of the studies focus on very specific clinical use cases for telemedicine or digitally enhanced virtual care services (e.g., telemedicine in diabetic foot ulcer management). Many researchers study the intervention in a specific non-generalizable population. This issue in the research makes the development of sweeping conclusions about telemedicine, or virtual care, generally difficult to make. As with any clinical intervention, generalizability from the setting and population of the study to other settings is often difficult and should not be done.

Despite inherent research challenges, there have been attempts to quantify the cost-effectiveness of telemedicine interventions as compared to existing standards of care. In one such systematic review article by Eze et al., cost-effectiveness was reviewed across 18 available studies.

It is conceptually easy to suggest that telemedicine may reduce the demand for face-to-face care. This article cites some evidence that direct-to-consumer telemedicine can sometimes be used in addition to in-person services and therefore could also increase the utilization of health services. Otherwise, it is more likely that certain telemedicine services would replace a face-to-face interaction, thus producing a comparable cost outcome.

As for the full review,[7] the authors found that 7 out of the 18 (39%) reviews evaluating cost-effectiveness found that that telemedicine interventions were cost-effective or cost-saving compared to the standard of care. Five out of 18 reviews (28%) found that telemedicine *could be* cost-effective or cost-saving—meaning they found statistically insignificant results. Two out of 18 reviews (11%) were unable to arrive at a robust conclusion. Four out of 18 reviews (22%) found that telemedicine was not cost-effective compared to standard of care. While most articles cite positive conclusions, the cost-effectiveness of telemedicine likely depends on the setting of care, how it fits into the overall clinical program, and how effectively the program is managed. In my opinion, given reasonable use, the outcome is likely equivalent in cost to in-person care when thinking about traditional audio-visual-based models.

Looking into further examples, one study[8] looking at cost-effectiveness of telehealth used for providing services to home care patients found that telehealth was not statistically significantly different versus standard home care for a number of factors that span clinical quality, cost, and patient experience.

The findings from this home care study suggest that telehealth services provided to patients in the home were equivalent to in-person care with respect to quality of life, psychological wellbeing, activities of daily living, mental health, and some disease-specific health outcomes. With relevance to cost, this same study found that telehealth and in-person services were equivalent for the number of inpatient days in the study population at 3, 6, 9 and 12 months. Evidence from this study also suggests that patients valued the telehealth services with findings that showed benefits to peace of mind and perceived access to healthcare.

Indeed, yet another review[9] looked at the cost-effectiveness and diagnostic accuracy of telemedicine in diabetic retinopathy and macular disease—common complications from diabetes. The authors found that the diagnostic accuracy is good. With respect to cost, teleretinal screening services, broadly, are cost-effective and reduced clinical workload for in-person clinics.

Finally, Farabi and colleagues performed a systematic review[10] looking at telemedicine in highly prevalent cardiovascular diseases—the leading cause of death in much of the developed world. The authors found that telemedicine improves clinical outcomes, and its use can result in considerable overall cost savings compared to usual care.

Furthermore, when telemedicine is utilized at the same time as usual face-to-face care, the effect is even more cost-effective when factoring overall patient service utilization.[11] This is one of the potential benefits of improved access to care and the development of high-touch telemedicine models—and one of the goals of the digital health movement, generally. While the cost of additional telemedicine touchpoints may exceed the cost of usual care when used in combination, if these lower-cost services can prevent costly episodes of care like emergency department visits or inpatient care, then telemedicine can represent a powerful intervention moving forward.

PATIENT SATISFACTION

From a review study[12] on telemedicine in the OECD, patient satisfaction was also broadly assessed. Fifteen reviews included in the study focused on patient experiences with telemedicine.

Six reviews addressed patient acceptability of telemedicine. All six studies found that patients found telemedicine acceptable for their healthcare service needs. The authors found that these outcomes had some variation based on patient population characteristics such as urban versus rural, age, gender, and socioeconomic status.

Six reviews included in the systematic analysis addressed patient satisfaction. Patients across all studies reported that telemedicine, and some other virtual care interventions, were convenient. Additionally, patients felt that these models of care foster independence and reassurance on their health because of a reduced burden and the perceived safety net of easily accessible telemedicine services.

Interestingly, the authors indicate that research suggests a higher level of telemedicine acceptability in patient populations than among groups of healthcare professionals and physicians. This is consistent with the resistance experienced by Dr. Boxer and the early pioneers which remains a barrier to adoption to this day. It also suggests that in a market-based health system like the US, consumer preferences and demand will drive the future of care delivery. Thus, given patient interest, healthcare organizations will have to adapt or face loss of market share.

**

Many factors should be carefully considered when weighing the evidence of telemedicine's efficacy, including specific intervention modality and care model, evidence of quality, and studied population demographics.

The definitional issues in the field cause major issues with respect to public awareness, policymaking, implementation, and continued research. For organizational decision-makers or policymakers evaluating digital health interventions, the lack of consistent terminology may inhibit positive actions to facilitate adoption. Any one of the following terms can refer to the same clinical intervention: telemedicine, RPM, virtual care, connected-care technologies, telehealth, or digital health program.

Does a video conference intervention between a physician and patient yield the same results as the same interaction that incorporates remotely collected blood glucose data? Does adding a health coach or patient educator to an RPM intervention improve patient outcomes? Does RPM provide more benefit than a video conference with a nurse biweekly? Does a full-virtual clinic for hypertension have better results than a hybrid RPM program? These questions can and have begun to be answered, but standardizing terminology will be essential moving forward.

Health services, and the institutional inertia driving many decisions within the industry, are often viewed differently than specific and targeted interventions like pharmaceutical products. However, as technology allows clinical models to get more specific to patients, it will become critical for clear program descriptions and well-designed clinical trials to dominate the discussion for the future of telemedicine and other virtual care models. This is a crucial step to continue advancing the field.

Equivalency has been established between audio-visual clinical models and in-person services. But, in the years after, new questions have emerged. Can we build virtual clinics that perform better than in-person services? Can we build the most patient-centric clinic using digital tools? Can we improve patient self-management with personalized delivery of education at scale? Can digital technologies improve the performance of human clinicians? Can we use technology to exceed the capabilities of in-person health services with respect to health outcomes and cost of care? Can we make healthcare services truly proactive? Can we use technology to make us healthier?

To do this, telemedicine providers are expanding scope of practice to address the most important and costly illnesses. Diabetes, heart disease, cancers, infectious diseases, and other chronic conditions that require continued care, behavior and lifestyle changes, and data-driven care must be addressed.

Fortunately, as smartphones have advanced so too have medical devices, physiological monitoring tools, and fitness trackers—measuring key metrics associated with individual behavior and health. Now, with a proven and accepted model of audio-visual telemedicine, those organizations advancing innovative digitally driven care have their sights set on not just meeting but exceeding the performance of traditional care delivery models. Telemedicine is just the beginning of a rapid push for not just more accessible access to health services but services that are more effective by touching factors not traditionally included in the medical model. Socioeconomic factors, environmental factors, and individual behaviors[13] are in in the sights of innovators pushing the bounds of digital health.

NOTES

1. They have since expanded due to an acquisition of Livongo Health in 2020. This acquisition marks a clear direction for the company that is the expansion of their scope of practice into highly prevalent chronic diseases.
2. Though some might argue this falls under public health and that medical care should be reserved for acute conditions.
3. Yet, doctors are trained that 80% of all diagnoses are obtained from the patient's history.

4. Note the term used by the authors. Here, once again, we can see the terminology issues that exist in the field. This review uses the term "telehealth" to refer to a wide range of clinical models and technologies, including live video conferencing. Once again, while "telehealth" and "virtual care" are likely broader synonymous terms, telemedicine typically refers to medical services rendered by a physician.

5. E. Shigekawa, M. Fix, G. Corbett, D. H. Roby, and J. Coffman. "The Current State Of Telehealth Evidence: A Rapid Review." *Health Affairs,* 37(12) (2018): 1975–1982. https://doi.org/10.1377/hlthaff.2018.05132

6. The authors excluded telephonic care management activities from nurses and social workers.

7. N. D. Eze, C. Mateus, and T. Cravo Oliveira Hashiguchi. "Telemedicine in the OECD: An Umbrella Review of Clinical and Cost-effectiveness, Patient Experience and Implementation." *PLoS ONE,* 15(8) (2020): e0237585. https://doi.org/10.1371/journal.pone.0237585

8. S. McFarland, A. Coufopoulos, and D. Lycett. "The Effect of Telehealth versus Usual Care for Home Care Patients with Long Term Conditions: A Systematic Review and Meta-analysis and Qualitative Synthesis." *Journal of Telemedicine and Telecare* (2019). https://dx.doi.org/10.1177/1357633X19862956

9. W. Ullah, S. K. Pathan, A. Panchal, S. Anandan, K. Saleem, Y. Sattar, E. Ahmad, M. Mukhtar, and H. Nawaz. "Cost-effectiveness and Diagnostic Accuracy of Telemedicine in Macular Disease and Diabetic Retinopathy: A Systematic Review and Meta-analysis." *Medicine,* 99(25) (2020): e20306. https://doi.org/10.1097/MD.0000000000020306

10. H. Farabi, A. Rezapour, R. Jahangiri, et al. "Economic Evaluation of the Utilization of Telemedicine for Patients with Cardiovascular Disease: A Systematic Review." *Heart Failure Review* (2019). https://doi.org/10.1007/s10741-019-09864-4

11. Ibid., 91.

12. N. D. Eze, C. Mateus, and T. Cravo Oliveira Hashiguchi. "Telemedicine in the OECD: An Umbrella Review of Clinical and Cost-effectiveness, Patient Experience and Implementation." *PLoS ONE,* 15(8) (2020): e0237585. https://doi.org/10.1371/journal.pone.0237585

13. I would also argue that genetics are also in the sights of precision medicine innovations. This type of innovation likely will have an impact for highly specialized treatment regimens and the selection of therapeutics, but this approach will not impact the important socioeconomic and individual behavior categories of health outcome drivers.

8

The Patient Relationship: The Softer Side of Virtual Care

I logged into the video conference application to find a very well-put-together and exquisitely dressed person on the other end of the call. During the Covid-19 pandemic, Zoom calls had begun to consume a large portion of the work day.[1] After several months of working, living, sleeping, and eating in the same place, the general work-from-home community was starting to get pretty casual as haircuts had been postponed and t-shirts started to dominate the workplace attire. But not this time.

Despite the circumstances, Dr. Faisel Syed presented a polished image and an even more polished *presence* over video conference. His clear intentionality about his presentation was immediately clear, and the contrast with other Zoom meetings was evident. Appearance aside, the uniqueness of his presence was derived from his general demeanor and interaction with the camera.

As the head of primary care at ChenMed, Dr. Syed is responsible for leading physician recruitment and primary care efforts at the clinic that operates in 10+ states. ChenMed is one of the only self-funded clinics that operates exclusively in full-risk arrangements with payors.[2]

ChenMed is fully responsible for the overall cost and quality of care for their patients. This is especially significant because they care for primarily Medicare patients aged 65 and older—the oldest, sickest, and costliest patients in the US healthcare system and in systems around the world. ChenMed's mission, as described by Dr. Syed, is to prove to physicians that extremely effective care for the frail older population is possible given the right approach, incentives, and clinical models.

The majority of healthcare providers and primary care clinics still operate under FFS payment models, but clinics like ChenMed accept full-risk arrangements and operate under a new clinical paradigm. For many in health policy and the payment side of healthcare, the pressure to control rapidly inflating healthcare costs is driving an aggressive push to value-based payment models that exist on a continuum from FFS through full-risk arrangements, like at ChenMed.

According to ChenMed[3]:

> ChenMed's doctors improve the health of the neediest seniors every day with our intensive high-touch care model. It's simple—when our patients do better, we do better. Each physician has a small patient panel that creates deep patient relationships with a focus on prevention. It's better for our patients, our doctors, and our success.

The current FFS payment models typically incentivize providers to maintain patient panel sizes of approximately 2,000 to 3,000 patients and to ensure roughly a high number of patient visits a day. But, when payment models shift from FFS to full-risk, the type of volume-driven, low-touch programs that are incentivized do not necessarily produce the results needed to control total cost or improve outcomes for patients. When any clinic takes on full-risk, something inherently needs to change in the way the clinical program is designed.

When I asked Dr. Syed about how ChenMed is able to control cost and improve outcomes for their patients, he made the answer very clear. It all comes down to establishing *trust*. ChenMed caps physician panel sizes at about 450 patients and encourages physicians to spend more time and effort developing and deepening patient relationships. It is safe to say that the ChenMed model exists on the far end of the spectrum from high-volume FFS primary care clinics. This is high-touch care that emphasizes the patient relationship to foster behavior change, to address socioeconomic factors, and to improve chronic disease outcomes.

At ChenMed, patients are seen once a month as opposed to every three months in most primary care settings. For more medically complex patients, visits are biweekly. Under the full-risk model, ChenMed is able to focus on the development of clinical programs that prevent costly emergency department visits, unnecessary care, costly prescriptions, and the impact of the social determinants of health.

This type of model is in direct contrast with the FFS model. Under FFS, provider behavior is dictated by the requirements to bill individual CPT codes. Each activity is then tied to a code, and the more codes that get billed the more revenue generated by the clinic. But these codes also place restrictions. There is variability between reimbursement rates tied to each code. Thus, clinics operating under this payment model select services that provide the highest reimbursement, which may not be the best fit for a particular patient.

Full-risk clinics, like ChenMed, have the cash on hand to ensure that they provide the right service to the right patient at the right time. Their hands are free to ensure that they meet the needs of each individual patient.

VIRTUAL CARE: THE DOCTOR–PATIENT RELATIONSHIP

For a physician who espouses the importance of the doctor–patient relationship in clinical practice and whose business model is entirely reliant on the effectiveness of their clinical models, I expected Dr. Syed to be a major critic of virtual and digitally delivered care. ChenMed is, after all, a high-touch care delivery model for our nation's *oldest* patients.

But, I was wrong.

"We had planned to roll out a virtual care strategy slowly over time, but Covid-19 caused us to speed up the implementation. In just 6 days, we had fully functioning virtual care programs stood up to provide services to our patients," said Dr. Syed, with usual enthusiasm.

During the Covid-19 pandemic, in-person clinical operations were suspended. Clinics, like ChenMed, were forced to accelerate their virtual care strategies that were already a part of their long-term strategic plan. Patient visits quickly shifted from in-person care to telemedicine with physicians visiting with patients via video conference.

Another criticism of telemedicine or virtual care as a whole, by physicians and others, is the perceived loss of the doctor–patient relationship.

The concern is valid and well placed. In-person interactions are unique, and the value of the emotional and empathetic communication that can be achieved through interpersonal interaction in person should not be discounted. Body language is an essential part of human communication.

It is important to recognize that virtual care will never replace the in-person patient visit for certain circumstances and services.

However, virtual care and services delivered via digital technology can also provide a patient–provider connection that is unique and distinct from that of an in-person interaction. There are two key benefits provided by virtual care in this sense:

> *Frequency of care:* The ability to extend services to patients more frequently due to the ease of virtual care technology access—in-person care is resource-intensive for patients (e.g., patient time, transportation, time off from work). For example, a patient who may be unlikely to come in for a needed second in-person visit may be more likely to accept a convenient virtual touchpoint with a provider.
>
> *Intimacy of care:* The virtual visit provides a unique experience for patients with their healthcare provider. The place of the visit is often in the home and reflective of the daily life of the patient.

"There is so much intimacy during a telemedicine or virtual care visit with a patient," explains Dr. Syed.

Dr. Syed, despite years of in-person-only care, has embraced the power of virtual care at ChenMed due to the access improvements, the unique engagement capabilities, and the ability to extend ChenMed's high-touch model to patients where a physical clinic is not located.

"I did a patient-initiation call via audio-visual telemedicine the other day with a patient in alcohol-abuse rehabilitation who was also homeless. He was unable to come into a clinic visit, but we had such an important conversation about his care and tendency to go to the emergency room when he needed a new prescription. I told him to send me a text when he needed a new prescription," recalled Dr. Syed.

In this case, the patient received access to his physician, Dr. Syed, and had an excellent experience using the telemedicine modality of care during a time when he could not attend in-person care. In this case, virtual care provided an important bridge to a high-risk patient, likely preventing an emergency department visit.

"Just this morning, I did a patient call with a 74-year-old woman who was sitting in her living room. The intimacy of that visit was incredible. This was her first audio-visual call, ever, and it happened to be with her physician—me. That is such an incredible experience for a patient to have the full attention of their physician in her living room," he explained.

Unlike in-person visits under FFS where a physician spends the majority of time entering notes into an Epic EMR facing away from the patient, Dr. Syed, on this virtual visit, was able to provide an intimate, focused encounter with the patient. Charting, under full-risk, becomes about recording important patient care information rather than burdensome billing documentation.

"She was ecstatic and enamored with the presence of her physician in her living room. I was able to ask her about her life, some of the items in view of the camera, and to engage with her in her own world," Dr. Syed continued.

While this is one physician's[4] experience with virtual care visits in a unique full-risk practice environment, Dr. Syed's experience can be made a universal one given the proper approaches to patient engagement and clinician presence via virtual care. Virtual modalities require shifts in demeanor and approach when it comes to interacting with patients.

For an especially engaged and professional physician like Dr. Syed to become a proponent of virtual care, the modality must demonstrate the ability to develop and maintain patient relationships. The research on this topic will continue to develop, but the physicians and clinical staff at ChenMed have figured it out. Outside of virtual care itself, ChenMed patients also receive a telephone call on a weekly basis to check in. At scale, these types of check-ins can be automated and scaled using digital technologies.

ChenMed is at-risk for the total cost of care for their attributed patients. If the clinic has implemented a specific intervention, then it *must* have value for patients and must be cost-effective. Patient engagement at ChenMed is an essential part of their model and, unbound by CPT codes, the providers of care have the freedom to interact with patients across a number of channels that work best for the patient.

TELEMENTAL HEALTH SERVICES: AN EXAMPLE OF VIRTUAL THERAPEUTIC RELATIONSHIPS

The "loss of relationship criticism" against virtual care services can be summarized as a disbelief that a healthcare provider is able build a therapeutic relationship with a patient over a video conference or phone interaction. This criticism is also firmly rooted in institutional inertia present in medicine, not necessarily in reality.

This belief that emotional connections and trust cannot be established via digital presence is not true. To some extent, it may be true that in-person interactions provide something more in terms of body language, the feeling of empathy, and the scope of services that can be delivered. Time, and research, will tell more about how patients and physicians interact in person versus virtually.

But we can look to the delivery of mental health services via audio-visual technologies as early evidence that this modality is not an inhibitor of the communication of empathy, trust, and the development of a strong therapeutic relationship.[5]

Mental health treatment through psychotherapy requires a clear level of trust and communication of empathy between provider and patient. Thus, the suitability of virtual care modalities in this clinical area can be used as an indicator of the potential for excellent patient interactions in other clinical domains, like chronic disease management.

The evidence suggests that telemental health services are equally effective as in-person therapy services. A Veterans Health Administration study[6] of telemental health services in older veterans shows positive outcomes compared to usual face-to-face care. Audio-visual-delivered psychotherapy for older adults with major depression shows equal performance with services provided to patients in the same room. This finding illustrates that evidence-based psychotherapy can be delivered, without significant modifications, via home-based audio-visual technologies. Importantly, this modality of care provides important access to people geographically distant from mental health providers and may be more acceptable to older adults than in-person care, which requires significant resources and commitment to attend. Indeed, there are well-established in-person therapy attendance issues in older adults.[7]

In another study[8] looking at patient perceptions of telemental health services, the evidence suggests that patients also express similar satisfaction with telemental health services when compared with usual care. A systematic review was performed to better understand patient-reported satisfaction with these care modalities. In this review of 14 studies, the findings suggest that patients are equally satisfied and rate provider–patient relationships equally between in-person care and audio-visual technology–facilitated.

Indeed, the power of virtual care tools in mental health treatment became increasingly evident during the Covid-19 pandemic in 2020. In an analysis[9] performed by Fair Health, deep in the midst of the Covid-19 pandemic in June 2020, 43% of all telemedicine visits were for mental health indications like depression and anxiety. Telemedicine claims, in general, jumped 4,131% from 2019 to 2020 due to the need to deliver care remotely to reduce the spread of the disease.

The elements required for effective patient engagement, namely the establishment of an empathetic therapeutic relationship, can be delivered via a virtual care medium at scale given sufficient training and intentionality by providers. In fact, it may be the case that certain elements can be delivered more effectively due to the unique aspects of virtual care. Services delivered through a patient's smartphone into the comfort of their home may contribute to an increased intimacy of the interaction—especially among older adults with whom technology use may be for mostly medical or family purposes. The access and attendance benefits from this care modality is also clear in the research and in anecdotal evidence from early clinician-adopters.

THE THREE ELEMENTS OF PATIENT ENGAGEMENT

There are several approaches to psychotherapy, but the most dominant is cognitive-behavioral therapy (CBT). In both mental and physical healthcare services, CBT principles are essential to the therapeutic relationship and in the development of engaging patient care programs. Thus, the comparison between telemental health services and those offered to patients with physical health ailments like diabetes and hypertension is valid, as the subjective goals of care like patient self-efficacy and behavior change are important in both condition groups.

For patients receiving low-stakes acute care like that offered by Teladoc and other direct-to-consumer telemedicine providers, the relationship with the provider and level of engagement with care is less important than for a patient receiving care for a chronic condition where a care plan must be consistently followed and altered based on the patient's condition over time.

It is widely acknowledged that the "holy grail" of effective healthcare services is the improvement of self-management behaviors and self-efficacy among patients with chronic disease. Due to the worldwide pressures to improve health outcomes with shrinking budgets, it is hypothesized that patient self-management is the best way to efficiently improve health outcomes for highly prevalent and costly chronic conditions. Essentially, if a patient is able to either better self-manage their condition or maintain positive health behaviors that prevent the formation of chronic illness in the first place, then demand for services can be reduced and health outcomes are therefore improved. As virtual care programs are developed to support these goals, their design must reflect these important facets of effective chronic care.

The traditional in-person and FFS-based primary care model does a poor job of accomplishing the self-management goals because it fails at the three elements of patient engagement: cognitive, behavioral, and emotional.[10] These three elements are also the focus of some CBT-based interventions:

- *The behavioral element* (the patient's *activities and actions*): the actions of a patient in connection and with relation to managing their disease.
- *The cognitive element* (the patient's *knowledge* and health metrics): what the patient knows and understands about their disease and their care plan. This encompasses how the patient understands the disease is monitored and the risks associated with the future.
- *The emotional element* (the patient's *feelings*): how the patient feels about their condition and the potential risks associated with it.

Effective health education can appeal to the cognitive element of engagement. Behavioral elements such as the examples of care plan adherence, diet choices, physical activity levels, and smoking cessation can be affected by healthcare provider reinforcement through the use of behavioral strategies and health coaching models. Emotional elements are important, as they affect motivation and patient mental health, which can both impact physical health outcomes. All three of these elements require substantial time and levels of patient personalization that are not granted under typical chronic disease care due to FFS time pressures.

Good in-person services have all of these elements, but the true test of virtual care models will be the ability to more effectively engage patients under all three. Given the power of the smartphone to collect data, to engage patients, to provide educational materials, and to facilitate connection to healthcare providers, the future looks bright for digital tools supporting health system improvement in these three areas.

As innovators and healthcare organizations seek to adopt digital health tools and develop virtual care programs, it is essential that they analyze the impact of their interventions on these three elements of patient engagement.

If done properly, then the use of virtual care models and digital technologies goes beyond simply replicating services that could be performed in person. Digital tools can allow for the development of an even more engaging and patient-centric model of care for patients with chronic illness.

Just as social media, Google, and TikTok have optimized their offerings to enhance engagement and user utility, digital health services can capture patients' attention better than traditional in-person healthcare services. Importantly, the use of digital technologies allows for the real-time optimization of engagement through techniques such as A/B testing and real-time patient feedback. The combination of multi-function apps collecting real-time data and providing educational content, audio-visual coaching sessions with a healthcare provider, and an increased level of convenient access will allow virtual care models to succeed where traditional healthcare organizations have failed at chronic disease care—care that is especially reliant on personalization and success across emotional, behavioral, and cognitive engagement.

The evidence thus far suggests that, when done correctly, virtual care modalities can impact all three areas of patient engagement.[11] The scalability of these technologies and the ubiquity of smartphones in many populations will continue to support traditional healthcare organizations in enhancing existing models and the development of new more effective tools aimed at improving patient self-management and the proactive provision of healthcare services.

Person-to-person interactions are essential to good chronic disease management, but the power of modern medicine to accurately diagnose and monitor patient health metrics is still essential to the provision of health services. Thus, cold hard data still matters in modern healthcare.

NOTES

1. And book writing processes for that matter.
2. Full-risk models are the next generation of payment models. Provider organizations receive a capitated payment based on actuarily derived rates on a monthly basis from a payor. With this funding, providers are responsible for the cost and quality of care they provide to their panel of assigned patients.
3. HomePage. ChenMed Website. Accessed August 20, 2020.
4. Dr. Faisel Syed is also a unique personality and physician, in general. Thus, his success may not be generalizable to all providers. However, it illustrates the versatility of the virtual care technologies as a tool to provide a unique experience for patients. There is something beautiful about welcoming a healthcare provider into one's home.
5. There is a growing movement to integrate mental health and physical health treatment. It is becoming widely acknowledged that physical chronic illness can have tremendous impact on mental health and vice versa.
6. Leonard E. Egede, Ron Acierno, Rebecca G Knapp, Carl Lejuez, Melba Hernandez-Tejada, Elizabeth H. Payne, B. Christopher Frueh. "Psychotherapy for Depression in Older Veterans via Telemedicine: A Randomised, Open-label, Non-inferiority Trial." *The Lancet Psychiatry*, 2(8) (2015): 693–701. ISSN 2215-0366. https://doi.org/10.1016/S2215-0366(15)00122-4.
7. Ibid., 100.
8. Michael A. Jenkins-Guarnieri, Larry D. Pruitt, David D. Luxton, and Kristine Johnson. "Patient Perceptions of Telemental Health: Systematic Review of Direct Comparisons to In-Person Psychotherapeutic Treatments." *Telemedicine and e-Health* (August 2015): 652–660. http://doi.org/10.1089/tmj.2014.0165
9. Monthly Telehealth Regional Tracker. July, 2020. FAIR Health. Online.
10. S. Barello, S. Triberti, G. Graffigna, C. Libreri, S. Serino, J. Hibbard, and G. Riva. "EHealth for Patient Engagement: A Systematic Review." *Frontiers in Psychology,* 6 (2016). https://doi.org/10.3389/fpsyg.2015.02013
11. Ibid.

9

Data Collection in Healthcare: An Overview

The Economist[1] released an article in 2017 that was titled, "The World's Most Valuable Resource Is No Longer Oil, but Data." Data, that is, on the global population. Our purchases, our genomic profiles, our physical attributes, our preferences, our demographic information, our incomes, our taxes, our app usage, the type of mobile device we have, our Internet use, and our favorite online shopping locations are all stored, analyzed, and sold.

Today, digital communication and information access are a baseline rather than something radical. You can order food from any establishment and have it at your door in 30 minutes from your mobile phone, you can stream every movie ever made to your TV without having to leave your couch, you can send money around the world using an email address, you can buy stock shares in a company in Japan instantly, you can invest in the Euro from a beach in the Cayman Islands, you can buy a currency that is "mined" using computers from your cellphone and send it to someone to purchase goods and services, you can become famous around the world on social media without even leaving your bed, and you can see what is happening at the corner of Pennsylvania Avenue from your friend who is visiting Washington, D.C., for the weekend. We live in the information age, where answers,[2] images, and media can be found anywhere at any time.

Why do we not have these experiences in healthcare? Modern medicine is a highly data-driven science, so it would follow logically that our institutions should unlock the data collected to make it more actionable, accessible, and helpful. Data collected by healthcare organizations is highly sensitive and well protected by several major federal regulations, but it can be stored and safely utilized given the proper safety protocols. To a large extent, the data has not yet been well connected to the patient experience outside of interactions within a physical location with a human healthcare provider. Patients, by and large, have not had access to their own health data and have had limited ability to cognitively associate their own behaviors with their health status.

In an industry where timely information literally saves or ends lives, the healthcare system has done a poor job of information management and access. Despite a whole generation growing up and utilizing the healthcare system in the midst of the global digital revolution, the industry as a whole is far behind in the widespread adoption of this technology.

Only due to government incentives and disincentives stemming from the Affordable Care Act in the US, healthcare organizations accepted the adoption of the electronic health record (EHR). At a fundamental level, this began healthcare's adoption of new digital health technology and has set the stage for the next generation of technologies and clinical models. Unfortunately, overall, the EHR has done little more than transfer medical records from paper to electronic. Indeed, after a lengthy search for evidence that EHRs improve clinical outcomes, I found none.

THE EHR

I would be remiss if, in a book about virtual care, I did not mention the foundational importance of the EHR. The transition from paper medical records to electronic health records is one that is fraught with challenges and resistance, and that has worsened burnout rates among clinicians.[3] These central repositories for patient records have transformed into a workflow facilitator and FFS billing engine that squeeze out as much productivity as possible from clinicians and drives revenue generation.

The efforts to digitize the medical record are well intentioned. The concept of unlocking patient data to enhance sharing among providers, to allow for better analytics, and to improve the efficiency of healthcare organizations is a good one. Unfortunately, the EHR story during the early 21st century is one that provides a textbook case of negative externalities and unintended consequences.

Recent research[4] suggests that by 2008, 73% of US hospitals had begun the transition to an EHR system. The US government, along with others around the world, pushed healthcare organizations or their government-sponsored system to modernize with these technologies. As with anything, this transition has taken time and iterations to achieve the end goal. I am confident that the shift to the EHR will yield tremendous gains in the next decade. However, this will likely be due to the innovations that are built off of this central patient record repository rather than due to the EHR itself.

The fact that the EHR was built for facilities to bill for services under FFS payment is the primary reason that these technologies have done little to impact patient outcomes at large.[5] This goes back to the genesis of the EHR wherein it was built for the customer—the healthcare organization and not the patient. Patient access to their data was an afterthought of most EHR designers.

For several years, I carried with me a belief that the adoption of the EHR was improving the quality of care across the country and world. At one point, I argued this exact point in a debate with a physician. As usual, I turned to Google Scholar to find supporting evidence for my thesis. I quickly came to the realization that I was wrong. At large, the widespread implementation of the EHR has not resulted in the corresponding gains in patient outcomes that had been theorized.

It does not take too much digging to discover why this may be the case. One of the largest companies in the EHR space is Epic Systems. Data publicized by Epic suggests that their view of the use of health information technology (HIT) remains driven by a facility-focused lens and billing concept. CEO Judy Faulkner suggested in an interview that of the 164 million patients with records in an Epic EHR, roughly 0.5% of them have downloaded the patient-facing app, MyChart, to view their own health records. Due to this information, Judy concluded that patients are not interested in managing or accessing their own health information, but rather they desire the health system to manage it for them.

These assertions are right in line with expectations and the clear lack of interest from Epic, and similar companies, in actually improving the effectiveness of healthcare services. It also reflects an inherent acceptance of the status quo in healthcare that historically shies away from models of care that can truly impact the experience of the patient because they are different than traditional models of face-to-face and transactional healthcare. Whether driven by profit motive or simply the high barrier that is the institutional inertia of healthcare, these beliefs are a continuation of attitudes that inhibit progress toward a more patient-centered and effective healthcare system.

The positive note here is that due to recent regulatory action to promote data sharing and patient access, there is now an open opportunity for new digital health technologies to bridge the gap between the health system's EHR and the patient.

THE EHR AND VIRTUAL CARE

Virtual care relies on technologies to enable patient access and clinician workflows by facilitating the transmission of data and communication between a healthcare organization and patients via digital technologies. As opposed to the organization-facing EHR, virtual care models rely on an IT infrastructure that connects the patient, and their data, to their care team. At this point, the EHR may receive outputs from these systems for storage, but it functions in the background as the documentation repository. Just as in a face-to-face encounter, there is patient data generated from virtual interactions or from connected medical devices as with RPM programs. It is important that this information is incorporated into the patient record, but given its real-time nature, it enables more proactive clinical models that EHR systems are not built to sustain currently.

This brings up an important point that underscores the connection between HIT and patient outcomes—a point that is missed by an EHR-only strategy. Here is that point: collecting and storing patient data does nothing unless it is acted upon by a clinician or a patient in a way that is meaningful for the patient and impactful on health.

In a face-to-face model utilizing an EHR, this interaction is limited temporally and spatially. In an advanced virtual care scenario, this information becomes accessible and actionable, continuously. Face-to-face models of care reflect a cross-sectional view of health due to data collection at infrequent periods and at a specific point in time. Virtual care models that leverage RPM can reflect the patient experience with health—that is, continuous and at all locations. This mindset has the potential to shift the conversation toward a more patient-centric use of HIT.

The challenges surrounding the adoption of the EHR, unfortunately, are major inhibitors to meaningful adoption of patient-facing mobile app technologies that are required for virtual care. EHRs have spawned a technology aversion among clinicians and have instilled a high-cost notion among administrators.

Judy Faulkner and Epic show a flawed understanding or purposeful ignorance of the patient experience. Patients have a deep desire and inherent motivation to understand and improve their health. A simple conversation with a few patients would lead the folks at Epic to understand that patients, in the current system, are left adrift in a sea of uncertainty regarding their care and health status.

We know that engaged patients have better health outcomes than those who are not and that engagement requires that patients understand their own health and the behaviors that they can adopt to improve it. The failures of MyChart adoption reflect a failure to design the patient-facing interface in a way that meaningfully reflects patient needs and that represents a tool for the proactive pursuit of health rather than the historical view of esoteric clinic-collected data.

This is where RPM and patient-generated data utilized as a part of a full virtual care model will succeed where Epic and MyChart have failed.

PATIENT-GENERATED HEALTH DATA (PGHD) AND WEARABLES

The term *patient-generated health data* has become the technical term used to refer to data collected or reported by patients themselves. In reality, *all* data collected in healthcare originates at the patient and thus this term is really a continuation of the same concept that the health system is the arbiter of patient health information rather than patients themselves. Furthermore, this concept is rooted in medicine's deep paternalism that views the physician in a position of power and authority over the patient rather than a partner in a health journey. While there is a need to differentiate the data collected and produced by patients and a clinician due to potential irregularities and measurement error, I argue that PGHD will be the major driver of virtual care's success.

The growth of the internet and wireless technologies has accelerated the development of devices that can measure physiological processes and other human-linked data. Bluetooth and Internet of Things technologies have further allowed this data to be integrated seamlessly into software applications and mobile devices.

The growth of consumer-focused medical devices, fitness trackers, and other medical-grade wearables has led to the realistic possibility that RPM clinical models can be scaled. These models, at a basic level, involve the remote collection and transmission of patient-generated data to a healthcare provider in near-real time. This new source of data expands the capabilities of healthcare organizations and represents an untapped resource in the current EHR-based clinical strategy. New digital health companies with technologies to bridge the gap between the patient and the care teams often provide an integration point to ensure that the patient-generated data finds its way into the patient's core EHR.

NOTES

1. "The World's Most Valuable Resource Is No Longer Oil, but Data." *The Economist.* The Economist Newspaper. May 6, 2017 Edition.
2. Note: Answers found on the internet are not always factual or based in science. To quote Descartes, "doubt everything."
3. I say this from personal experience speaking with clinicians who attribute their burnout to the use of the EHR. This is also well substantiated in the clinical and medical informatics literature.
4. Jordan Everson, Joshua C. Rubin, and Charles P. Friedman. "Reconsidering Hospital EHR Adoption at the Dawn of HITECH: Implications of the Reported 9% Adoption of a 'Basic' EHR." *Journal of the American Medical Informatics Association,* 27(8) (August 2020): 1198–1205. https://doi.org/10.1093/jamia/ocaa090
5. This statement is made based on a scientific literature review. There are likely certain programs or use cases that have produced benefits for patient safety and patient outcomes. However, the EHR has mostly reinforced FFS-driven incentives that do not reflect the best clinical models for most patients.

10

Wearables and Predictive Analytics

Reacting quicker to an airplane that crashed is not as important as predicting that a crash will happen.

—Gerald Wilmink, PhD, Chief Business Officer at CarePredict

**

"My parents got divorced when I was 10, so I moved in with my grandfather, who was like my dad," said Jerry Wilmink as he started to tell me about his career journey. Like many innovators and entrepreneurs I interview, Jerry immediately began his professional story with his childhood. For people who dedicate their lives to the risky, unstable, and uncertain business of innovative start-up companies, there is often a higher purpose driving their actions.

"My grandfather, who was in his mid-70s, suffered from Lewy body Dementia, which is somewhere in between Alzheimer's and dementia," explained Jerry.

From an early age, Jerry Wilmink was exposed to the challenges of chronic illness. As he grew up, he would attend Vanderbilt University, in Nashville, Tennessee, where he would study biomedical engineering in both undergrad and, eventually, through the completion of a doctoral program.

Now, as Jerry Wilmink, PhD, he would go on to set up a new spectroscopy lab for the Department of Defense (DoD) and come to manage the Air Force SBIR grant program—a program often leveraged by start-ups to gain initial R&D funding. Part innovation accelerator, part venture-capital organization, the SBIR program is a major federal initiative to promote innovation and research across the different federal agencies including at the National Institutes of Health.

During his time at the DoD, Jerry would come to learn how much he enjoyed building things from scratch and would go on to publish scientific papers, begin an executive MBA program, and come to understand the level to which bureaucracy and slow-moving innovation brings him down. The combination between his professional experiences during this time and a personal life event would inspire Jerry to leave his stable, tenure-track position to pursue solutions that truly solve tangible problems.

"My grandfather, again suffering from his dementia, fell in route from his bedroom to the bathroom. He laid there for hours until my grandma found him. He ended up living through that event but passed away not too long after in 2010."

Jerry credits this episode and subsequent loss of the man who raised him as the catalyst for wanting to do something to solve the problem of falls for older adults.

*

Healthcare is full of data sets that already exist and are unused or underused by organizations. Developing solutions and products that leverage these existing sets of data will continue to dominate the world of digital health technology. But as mobile products and technologies continue to dominate the consumer landscape, the ability to collect never-before-available data now exists—that is PGHD.

But data collected for the sake of collecting data is not particularly useful. In order to help transform the delivery of care to a more proactive orientation, something needs to be done with that data to transform it into information and knowledge and to make it actionable for patients, caregivers, and care teams.

Given available data, there has been a great deal of interest in the use of advanced analytics and artificial intelligence to better predict outcomes and to assign risk to patients. Once existing data or PGHD is collected, the ability to identify and flag risk factors for specific outcomes becomes available. This is one of the future iterations of RPM-based technologies—the assignment of real-time risk scores for outcomes like emergency department visits, hospitalization, falls, or general condition exacerbation.

For Jerry, motivated by personal life experience, the natural place to look for ways to better collect and leverage data was to patients. Leveraging his engineering experience and expertise, Jerry set out to solve the problem he witnessed firsthand. He looked at solutions that already existed on the market and discovered that most fall-related senior technologies helped people call for help and to receive help more quickly once they have already fallen.

"Reacting quicker to an airplane that crashed is not nearly as important as predicting that a crash will happen," quipped Jerry.

Jerry looked at the existing technologies and decided that it would be ideal if the technologies could pick up behaviors that precluded a fall. Rather than simply facilitating a response to a fall, Jerry wanted to have wearable technologies that can alert the patient and others that a fall was imminent.

Thus, Jerry founded WiseWear, a company that developed biosensing wearables that can predict falls and other important health outcomes for patients in the home. Jerry raised $8 million in venture funding to develop the technologies and enlisted technology experts and fashion designers to bring his vision to life.

"We had a hearing aid that could detect balance and collect data, but we needed to raise more money to bring it to market after it was developed."

That is around the time when Jerry was introduced to Satish Movva, the CEO and founder of CarePredict. Satish was motivated by a similar story to Jerry—a family experience that prompted him to seek the ability to prevent bad patient outcomes before they happen.

Satish developed the first electronic medical record for the Palm Pilot and original SaaS platforms for the home care and home health industries before starting CarePredict, after caring for his mother and father residing in their own home. After a few emergency department visits with his parents, Satish, like Jerry, realized there was a need for more advanced technologies in the space.

After looking at existing products on the market, like ambient motion sensors that could be placed on refrigerators or on beds to monitor activity, Satish realized that there were two key problems with existing technologies. One, these sensors did not produce patient-specific data that could be linked to any one individual. And two, these sensors were unable to determine whether the motion was created by Mom and Dad going about their lives in a healthy, happy manner or simply the dog walking around.

"He knew that wasn't enough," said Jerry, as he drew the parallels to his own story with WiseWear.

In order to help solve the problems associated with older adults living at home on their own, both Jerry and Satish knew that new devices were necessary. Satish founded CarePredict in 2013, the first to market with a solution that detects changes in daily activities and predicts potential issues like falls, urinary tract infections, depression, and malnutrition. In 2018, CarePredict purchased Jerry's WiseWear.

"CarePredict collects the most accurate data on activity and behavior, and changes to these, we know, are precursors to a health decline," Jerry continued.

Thus, the resulting combined product produced by CarePredict has been on the market for several years now in both the US and Japan. And it works exceptionally well. The product is a wrist-based wearable device that is worn by an individual to understand and analyze their activities of daily living. The system collects motion and other biosensed data from the wearer and compiles it into a profile that establishes a baseline of normal activity. Items like the individual's personalized drinking gesture, personalized eating gesture, how they wash their face, the room they are in, and how they bathe are all measured and a baseline of "normal" is established. With the established health baseline for activities, the ability to predict or identify risk for certain outcomes is possible.

The CarePredict platform is extremely well suited for and performs well when predicting falls. If an individual's activities and motion begins to deviate in such a way from the baseline that shows instability—that individual is flagged as being at a higher fall risk.

"We can predict and identify individuals [who] are at risk for and experiencing depression. If we see a decrease in baseline activity levels, reductions in social time where the individual is spending time alone instead of in the community, and eating durations decreased from the longitudinal baseline; we identify that individual as potentially depressed," explained Jerry.

CarePredict is already seeing fast adoption in the home care space. It has been adopted by the largest provider of home care services in Japan and has raised $18 million in venture funding. The company is doing well, and their technology has undoubtedly saved patients and families from the suffering associated with falls and subsequent emergency department experiences.

CarePredict was originally piloted in senior living facilities to enable the program to learn and have the support of staff during the study period.

According to Jerry, who is looking to publish the results in a peer-reviewed journal, the solution has reduced hospitalizations by 27%, increased staff response time by 27% to 41%, and decreased monthly fall rates by 37%, and the average length of stay for the individual in the assisted living facility, rather than involving deterioration requiring transfer to a skilled nursing facility, increased.

These types of predictive solutions can have a major patient health and financial impact. Preventing hospitalizations can cut costs by tens of thousands of dollars, decreasing falls prevents the suffering and subsequent health issues associated with them, and quality of life is improved by allowing individuals to remain in assisted living rather than in a hospital bed in a skilled nursing facility.

The benefit of wearable monitoring technologies like those of CarePredict's program is that data is collected passively. The best technologies add value, solve problems, and often work passively. The patient simply has to wear the device and it works after an initial setup period. There is not significant user input. This makes this device relatively accessible and useable by anyone who can wear it on their wrist. For digital health, user engagement metrics are essential to success. High rates of user time spent using the product and longer user retention metrics are essential to the success of products.

Importantly, the data collected is analyzed and presented to patients, caregivers, and care teams to allow for actionable insights. The information is visualized and flagged in real time to actually impact patient care rather than simply storing the information in an EHR. In fact, CarePredict has become a central part of their customers' operations in assisted living. They are not simply a source of data, but rather something around which programs and operations are built.

"You cannot just do a data dump on the staff. Taking the data, making the predictions, and identifying the high-risk individuals is necessary," Jerry finished as he explained the importance of a holistic program built around the technology.

11

Remote-Patient Monitoring

It's not the monitoring that changes care, it is the collaboration and connection.

—Dr. Greg Weidner, MD, FACP

**

Dr. Greg Weidner, MD, FACP, is one of the early pioneers of the use of patient-centric digital technologies in primary care. His contributions to the modernization of health services are apparent across a number of organizations and most recently at the innovative digital health technology company Carium. As chief medical officer, he informed product design and clinical transformation for customers.

His foray into the world of digital health began roughly two decades earlier than our conversation. As a primary care physician and physician-executive at a large health system on the East Coast of the US, he traces his "digital health roots" back to his early days in quality improvement and medical informatics.

In 2004, he was tasked with leading the selection, implementation, optimization, and adoption of the health system's EHR. The movement toward EHR systems in healthcare prompted his health system to set about building a world-class enterprise clinical information system. After a wide search and evaluation process, the organization selected Cerner as their EMR vendor.

As medical director for the new initiative, the Canopy Electronic Medical Records Program, Dr. Weidner had a hand in the implementation across the enterprise from inpatient, to ambulatory, to emergency department. EHR implementation at a large integrated health system is a huge undertaking and involves people, process, and technology work across all roles and environments. Under Dr. Weidner's meticulous eye, the project was a fast success as the health system slowly transitioned from a paper-based system to the future of healthcare information technology.

But Dr. Weidner's medical training, clinical quality improvement background, and patient-centric design sensibility led him to ask important questions about the project. One of those questions was: how have we transformed care with the considerable money, time, and effort spent implementing this EHR system?

Around 2012, Dr. Weidner asked himself this question and came to the realization that the EHR system had not sufficiently impacted patient outcomes or experience of care for patients and care teams.

It quickly became clear to Dr. Weidner that the EHR was the foundation and not the end point as he began considering the future of medical informatics and technology's place in care delivery. Around this same time in 2012, a vision for the next frontier in care delivery came into view for Dr. Weidner. This vision involved extending the EHR infrastructure to redesign and transform care delivery models, an extension, that is, to patients and families as they navigate their care.

Beyond the EHR, which is built for the healthcare enterprise rather than the patient, Dr. Weidner knew that care delivery redesign efforts must begin to consider how to put technology into the hands of patients, caregivers, and families. According to Dr. Weidner, the next generation health IT infrastructure will consider patients, their families, and their care teams as the true end users, rather than the health system. In his role, he provided leadership to important incremental progress in this direction with solutions like a tethered enterprise patient portal, video visits, and asynchronous eVisits, but had a more ambitious design vision to support consumers and patients in their journey.

In pursuit of this grander vision, Dr. Weidner and colleagues approached the senior leadership at their health system with a bold plan.

"We pitched to the senior leadership the notion of creating a frontier scout team, to ride ahead and identify opportunities and challenges just as in the frontier wagon train days. In the end, this amounted to a prototyping primary care practice co-located with a design lab (the Center for Proactive Health and Design) under the same roof," explained Dr. Weidner.

The practice was commissioned as an emergent strategy innovation unit within the larger health system enterprise. In order to redesign care delivery in light of modern technology, they essentially built an agile primary care practice to develop and evaluate new models of care. Exploring the introduction of technologies and new staffing models, Dr. Weidner and the team set out to completely rethink the traditional way a primary care operates.

Dr. Weidner set out to build a *proactive* healthcare delivery model for patients with chronic disease. In his mind, the following three items were the central operating thesis for the R&D program:

1. To empower individuals in caring for their own health.
2. To enable patient care teams to become proactive rather than reactive.
3. To lead the health system toward defining the future of proactive health services.

"We moved very quickly and were able to get elbow to elbow and shoulder to shoulder insights directly from patients, families, and care teams," Dr. Weidner continued as he described their patient-focused development methodology.

Their first clinical pilot was focused on those living with and managing chronic conditions. In 2013, they did a six-month program with mHealth-enabled diabetes care. They initially enrolled 20 patients. Outfitted with mobile apps and better communication tools, the patients were monitored and connected with their care team remotely. Patient support included multidisciplinary care team touchpoints, remote blood glucose monitoring, and peer support.

This first evaluation was small, but the results were very positive. With respect to clinical outcomes, engagement, and the response from patients, the program was a success that demonstrated the potential for a larger program.

"Our patients did not want to go anywhere else or back to a traditional model of care. They asked us if they could keep doing this. Our care team could also feel the positive impact of this reimagined care on their patients and on their own professional satisfaction," he recalled. Self-efficacy, support, peace of mind, and added accountability were frequently mentioned by patients about their perceived value provided by this new model.

After the first minimum viable product was demonstrated, Dr. Weidner and team felt like they had the trappings for a new and scalable clinical care clinic. Thus, shortly after demonstrating success, they launched their first freestanding Proactive Health practice. The practice was a team-based, technology-enabled, whole-person model of value-based primary care.

"What I have talked about so far is not really RPM as you would think about it today—we wanted to figure out truly patient-centered care for patients rather than just adding a new box to check onto the traditional model or just to capture revenue," he mentioned as he referenced the section of the book of which he knew he was the center.

Dr. Weidner and the team did not specifically seek out RPM as a piece of their next-generation care delivery model. RPM became a part of the program because it was helpful in the context of a larger connected care clinical program—it was helpful for patients and care teams. Technology was also not the focal point of the program; rather it was assumed to be a major part of their work because it is the only way to efficiently facilitate the team-based care models they envisioned.

"Our mission was to extend and enhance the relationship that individuals have with their health and their healthcare teams," Weidner says. Technology was always assumed to be an enabler—to allow the model to be scalable, data-driven, personalized, and skill-optimized. RPM was a key component of a new patient-centered operating system for care."

After a good bit of R&D, their first freestanding Proactive Health clinic launched with a simple framework that guided their clinical activities. The goal was to completely redefine the patient experience of care by offering a program that addresses all three elements of effective patient engagement and to anticipate and provide for needs across the patient journey. Their program operated using the following framework:

1. Personalized assessments for patients.
2. Individualized care plan development.
3. Real-time support for patients in following their care plan.

The personalized assessment portion of the patient journey involved taking a holistic look at a patient's risk factors for their disease as well as individual goals and perspectives. Factors assessed included fitness, nutrition, sleep, stress, medical conditions, and social factors. This personalized risk assessment takes into consideration more factors than the typical medical model that exists today.

After the personalized assessment was performed, patients would be taken through a shared care plan development process to identify areas of opportunity for them to improve their self-management of their condition. Evidence-based behavior science was incorporated into the program design to help the care team facilitate health behavior change for patients.

The personalized assessment and shared-care planning processes are similar to, but more holistic than, those that occur in primary care settings around the world. But care delivery models for chronic illness often fall short at the point beyond the assessment and care plan development. This is the point at which Dr. Weidner's model far exceeds the typical allowing for more continuous engagement and support between office encounters and connecting within the fabric of patients' lives.

Patients would receive consistent and continuous support from their care team members remotely. Patients were sent home with a suite of digital tools to collect data and to enable continuous communication. Through collaborative messaging with the care team, patient care plans were adjusted as the RPM data indicated a change. Patients were offered access to a peer-to-peer network with group programs. The goal of the support program was to allow patients to connect with their own health, their care team as needed, and with each other. Protocols and program standardization allowed for an efficient and skill-optimized delivery approach for the care team.

This model was easily reproducible across a number of highly prevalent chronic conditions. Dr. Weidner indicated that they focused initially on diabetes, hypertension, and weight management. Specifically, in hypertension, he indicated that 81% of more than 500 patients enrolled made it to their clinical goal within 90 days. With a holistic focus on not just medical interventions but lifestyle ones as well, they were often able to de-escalate medications. According to Dr. Weidner, their quality metrics from the program put them among the top performers across the nation.

The success of the program likely comes from effective patient engagement that leads to holistic improvement of factors that impact a patient's health and a focus on proactivity. This model is a technologically focused cousin to the work done at ChenMed that is also a high-touch model that emphasizes patient engagement and the development of open communication between a care team and patients.

These models may be viewed with skepticism by CFOs and the business side of healthcare organizations due to the perceived scalability issues associated with high-touch care. This is the specific reason that technology and digital tools will continue to diffuse into clinical practice. These tools remove inefficiencies that have previously inhibited high-touch models of care. Through the automation of administrative and manual processes, digital tools can empower clinics to incorporate these connected care models into their workflows in ways that the EHR does not support. Such models require purpose-built tools for engagement, health behavior change, team-based care, and remote interaction via synchronous and asynchronous channels.

"As technology solutions advance in this arena, we will realize the value of automating the transactional while expanding the relational aspects of care," noted Dr. Weidner.

One of the other key areas needed for building a clinically successful and operationally sustainable proactive care practice is the ability to rely on multiple levels of clinicians. Digital technologies allow for certain patient interactions to be routed to the appropriate level. Sometimes, a patient concern can be routed to a medical assistant or health coach. Other times, a patient concern can be routed to a nurse, while others require the attention of an advanced care practitioner or physician. With thoughtfully designed technologies and accompanying processes, issues can often be anticipated, resolved, or queued up to the appropriate member of the care team for a personalized but highly scalable experience.

RPM: THE TECHNICAL DEFINITION

RPM has both a conceptual definition and a clear definition outlined by the CPT code billing requirements. These are the definitions outlined by the American Medical Association and reimbursed by the Centers for Medicare and Medicaid Services and other payors.

Conceptually, RPM is the use of information or communications technology to collect physiological, or other, data from patients when they are not physically located within a clinic. These programs, as already established, can span a wide range of conditions and programs.

TABLE 11.1

RPM CPT Codes and Medicare Reimbursement

		National AVG Rate
99453	Patient set up & education (1 time)	$ 19.46
99454	Remote transmission of data (monthly)	$ 64.15
99457	20 minutes of data review/ communication (monthly)	$ 51.54
99458	Additional 20 minutes of data review/ communication (monthly)	$ 42.22

The billing definition of RPM services follows the sequence of events outlined in Table 11.1.

The bare minimum for RPM services is the identification of a patient with coverage for RPM services. Patients are then enrolled into the program by their treating healthcare provider, informed about the program, and asked to provide consent.

At this point, the patient receives their devices or the technology used to perform the data transmission. Patient setup, or CPT code 99453, then is billed for education on the program one time. The supplied devices or technology (e.g., an app) must be an FDA-approved medical device that collects physiological data relevant to the patient's diagnosis—thus, a gray area is the ability to bill RPM for subjective patient data.

At this point, the patient goes home and is instructed to take their readings on a daily basis. CMS has set a minimum requirement for data transmission to ensure the patient is actually using the device—thus, RPM CPT code 99454 requires readings from about half the month in order to be billed. This means the patient must take a reading at least every other day for each month.

In a barebones RPM program, once the data transmission is occurring successfully, the treating provider or designated clinical staff must spend 20 minutes of time monthly reviewing the patient data and communicating treatment plan alterations with the patient. Once this requirement is met, then CPT code 99457 becomes available for billing. Each addition 20 minutes spent on a patient each month is billable via code 99458.

It is important to recognize that the simple act of data collection and compliance with these code requirements alone are likely not sufficient to provide clinical value to patients.

The billing requirements constitute the bare minimum for an RPM program. RPM, then, from a billing perspective can be accomplished with potentially limited benefit to patients if programs operate on a bare minimum approach that does not incorporate the data into a more robust program. Collecting data for the sake of doing so likely does little to benefit patients.

12

RPM-Driven Virtual Care: Frontline Perspectives

This is the care I want for my parents, my grandparents, and really it's appropriate for anyone with a chronic condition.

—Angie Stevens, RN, BSN

*

"I started my nursing career on a Cardiology unit," explained Angie as she started answering my first question during our interview.

I met Angie Stevens, RN, BSN, through my RPM research. I spent a month doing semi-structured qualitative interviews with anyone I could find who was involved with RPM. I talked to companies, nurses, physicians, researchers, and even patients. I was trying to understand the implementation of programs beyond what was available in the clinical literature, which often misses the softer, subjective elements of the programs evaluated. One of the best ways to gain a deeper understanding of RPM-based virtual care programs is to interview the people directly involved in caring for patients after performing a thorough literature review.

Angie, like many clinicians, at one point in her career, started questioning her role in the overall vision of healthcare. Like most nurses, she was trained to understand health as a holistic picture that involves individual behavior, socioeconomic, environmental, and traditional medical factors.

"I cared for patients before and after invasive cardiovascular procedures. The overwhelming trend of unhealthy lifestyles and habits was very evident. I felt called to find a role where I could educate patients proactively on lifestyle measures that would hopefully help prevent chronic conditions that led them to need these procedures," she continued.

"So, you realized that you weren't helping people attain and maintain better health, you were just reacting after a lifetime of poorly managed chronic illness," I concluded.

Angie spent a couple years working on the cardiology floor of a hospital and then made the jump into primary care, where she felt she was better able to support patients on a path to better health. And Angie did feel better in her new primary care setting, but after a few months began to search for even more opportunity to support her patients.

"I loved the primary care space; however, it was still difficult to fit in the educational elements that I had hoped for in the traditional fee-for-service model. We saw patients back-to-back and, as hard as we tried, we still had limited time to really dive into lifestyle habits and to create personalized action plans."

Even in primary care, Angie was bumping up against the volume-driven time constraints of FFS healthcare and the limitations of in-person-only healthcare services. While this is a book about virtual care, the reimbursement environment plays a pivotal role in how organizations deliver care. Fortunately, Angie met Dr. Greg Weidner, and she joined his new primary care practice experiment.

Dr. Weidner's search for something that can add value to primary care led him and Angie to connected care conferences where he met the team at Twine—one of the early digital health companies in the RPM and connected-care space. They adopted this new technology and, as Twine's first client, started running their pilots with patients.

"The outcomes from our first hypertension pilot were pretty remarkable and exciting, with favorable feedback from patients. We were able to get 81% of our patients' blood pressures controlled remotely within 90 days using RPM," said Angie.

Angie then pulled out some of the recorded outcomes from the program and proudly shared their success. According to their program evaluation, 93% of patients rated their pilot hypertension program as "very high quality" or "high quality." After demonstrating success in this first pilot, the team began designing programs for other chronic conditions such as diabetes, prediabetes, and weight management.

Success in a hypertension or diabetes treatment program means patient blood pressure and blood glucose become stable within a reasonable range. But true success is the deprescription of medication due to significant improvement. Due to the success of their program at achieving this outcome, Angie began reporting patients with deprescribed medications as a metric to illustrate their performance. Beyond reporting these uniquely successful metrics, the program consistently demonstrated top decile performance in the typical clinical quality metrics.

Angie lived this clinical model every day on the frontlines with patients. Beyond the clinical trials, the softer benefits of RPM come out when speaking to patients who participate in the program. It is essential to answer the question: what does this actually look like and how do patients respond to it?

"Managing patients' chronic conditions via RPM is a game-changer. We coached patients on lifestyle changes and saw real-time improvement in data as they modify their health habits," explained Angie.

Angie tells that providing patients with access to their own health data in real time allows for a number of important benefits. The most important is that patients can cognitively connect the impact of their lifestyle, medication, and other modifications to their own health in real time. This insight came directly and unprompted from Angie and is an example of the interplay between the cognitive and behavioral elements[1] of patient engagement in practice.

With RPM, Angie continued, patients do not need to bring 20 pages of paper with the last month's numbers to clinic visits. The data is available for use in the clinic in real time and by the patient at home. In current care standards, patients are often encouraged to monitor their own clinical data (e.g., blood pressure) frequently even without a connected-care technology. RPM allows for patients to do so digitally, often accompanied by easy-to-understand charts, and with transmission to their care team.

According to Angie, this feature of effective RPM programs helps patients feel empowered to affect their own health. This is an important distinction from the current standard of care, where healthcare providers stand in a position of power or paternalism over their patients rather than acting as partners. When healthcare providers control the source of patients tracking their progress and patient data, it does not facilitate patient engagement and empowerment.

Angie recalled an important story to illustrate the power of RPM in action—her favorite example. She described an insulin-dependent older adult widower, who lived at home alone. As per the program, he checked and logged his fasting blood glucose daily first thing in the morning. One of her first daily tasks each day for the RPM workflow was to check patient "alerts" in the morning to see whether anyone had any high or low readings that occurred in the overnight period. This particular patient would semi-frequently transmit a low blood sugar reading which would cause an "alert" flag. Upon seeing the alert, Angie would call him immediately to perform an assessment and provide new medication orders. On one occasion, this occurred, and he answered the phone with, "Hey Ang, want me to decrease my insulin by 2 units tonight?" He knew Angie would be calling, and, through his prior experience with the RPM program, he knew the action plan resulting from his low reading.

Beyond the educational and self-management benefits of RPM, Angie made clear that one of the most important outcomes from this type of program is the patient-reported outcome of improved peace of mind. She recalled that this was the most common feedback received from patients and their spouses, with the following as a typical comment: "I know you're watching my numbers and will call with a plan if you are concerned."

Importantly, Angie indicated that RPM programs also allow nurses to work at the top of their licenses, while decreasing physician workloads and burdens. When empowering highly educated clinicians, like nurses, to provide a higher level of care to patients as coaches and RPM leaders, physicians can focus on patients of higher complexity and on ensuring proper care plan design. In a world of overworked physicians, this could be a positive effect of the diffusion of robust RPM-based virtual care models.

ENGAGING OLDER ADULTS

When I talk to healthcare organizations or clinicians about smartphone-based clinical models like RPM, the most consistent question is about the ability of older adults to participate and engage with the program. In RPM, digital literacy as well as health literacy become two important factors to consider.

Given the high prevalence of chronic illnesses in the Medicare population and the reliable reimbursement for RPM service for Medicare patients, this patient population is a core focus for RPM care delivery models. Despite the availability, one of the largest criticisms of RPM is that older adults cannot or will not use it. The skeptics cite this as a major barrier to implementation and scalability of RPM monitoring programs.

"We learned that our 65+ patients are actually pretty savvy and were able to pick this up pretty easily. In many cases, just like us, they have their iPhones and they were already downloading apps. This was nothing they could not handle. Our oldest patient was 90 years old—and he was the first patient to use a new feature that Twine had added. The new feature enabled patients to send a picture over to us in the message part of the platform," Angie explained. "He had a rash one day and sent us a picture of it. I loved that he was the first patient to use the new feature," she noted.

Given sufficient education, healthcare provider encouragement, and motivation to learn to use an app-based RPM platform, a certain subset of older adults are able to succeed on these programs. In this same vein of thinking, Dr. Faisel Syed frequently jokes to both critics of and newcomers to virtual care that the older generation is the one that grew up with *The Jetsons*—they expected a form of technology that far exceeds the current modalities in healthcare. Thus, they can, without too much doubt, comprehend and adjust to this modality of care.

Angie mentioned that it was rare to find a patient who was unable to utilize the technology. Most of the patients they enrolled in the program were in their 60s, 70s, and 80s, with an average age of 62. At the peak of their program, they had 300 patients using the platform.

Older adults, in Angie's experience, were often retired and had plenty of time to engage with the program. They were actively involved and interested to learn a new technology and how to improve their health through diet, exercise, and other positive self-management behaviors.

As we wrapped up our discussion on older adults, Angie reminded me that many of her patients in the program were already on Facebook to keep up with their grandkids—so adding an RPM app for their health was not too much of a stretch for them. This does, however, stress the importance of user-centric design for applications that may be utilized by older adults. In short, keep them simple, relevant, and useful.

RPM: BEYOND PHYSIOLOGICAL DATA TRANSMISSION

When RPM is done right, according to Angie,[2] it transcends just data collection. The most effective RPM programs incorporate patient education and counseling as interventions.

"It is a form of counseling, remotely. Communicating and corresponding with patients about their health metrics and helping them develop an action plan was something many patients had never experienced before and something they liked," Angie continued.

Too often, RPM is viewed solely as the collection and transmission of data from patients. But, this is only one component of effective virtual care programs. When done right, RPM allows practices to extend office visits into the patient's daily life as an elongated clinic visit. This is the major objective of connected and virtual care models. Rather than short 15-minute, unpleasant clinical visits every three to four months, patients are able to learn and engage with their health continuously over time. It becomes a journey rather than a destination.

Angie shared that a strong RPM program provides the following benefits:

- The proactive management of chronic diseases in real time.
- Collecting true patient metrics to make medication decisions versus "white coat syndrome"[3] metrics.
- The continuous connection between patients and their care teams, allowing for long-term behavior change.
- The ability to watch metrics improve and to trigger medication change recommendations to physicians.

NOTES

1. S. Barello, S. Triberti, G. Graffigna, C. Libreri, S. Serino, J. Hibbard, and G. Riva. "EHealth for Patient Engagement: A Systematic Review." *Frontiers in Psychology*, 6 (2016). https://doi.org/10.3389/fpsyg.2015.02013
2. And as supported by the clinical literature.
3. This is a phenomenon that occurs frequently during the in-office measurement of blood pressure. Patient stress and other factors associated with the clinical environment can elevate blood pressure readings.

13

Remote-Patient Monitoring Outcomes

Does this even work?

—**A healthcare professional, somewhere**

**

The most frequent question asked by clinicians and healthcare organizations about RPM-focused virtual care programs is: does this even work?

The same critiques of early telemedicine via audio-visual technologies resurfaced as RPM models began to gain traction. The inability to touch the patient is still a concern for potential adopters. But RPM offers more than telemedicine alone. The collection of real-time clinical data from patients extends scope of practice from those sinus infections to chronic illness by providing data for clinical decisions and intervention selection.

From the period of 2010 to 2020, RPM technologies grew in number. As with anything, the marketing materials and narratives took many forms as companies seek product and program differentiation. Driven by both a lack of terminology standardization and sales strategy, those responsible for the implementation of new clinical models at health systems have been inundated with marketing materials that lack clarity and clear evidence.

For system-based clinical intervention models like RPM, as opposed to pharmaceutical interventions, the burden of evidence is lower with respect to regulatory oversight. Outside of HIPAA, there are few regulations that target service-facilitating apps that are not self-contained interventions (i.e., digital therapeutics). Thus, as fast as technologies can be developed, they can hit the market with little hindrance or clinical evidence requirements. Too often anecdotes trump clinical trials in new markets, and thus it is important to seek reliable sources of evidence when looking to develop a new RPM-based virtual care strategy.

The terminology issues, coupled with essentially limited regulatory oversight, have created a confusing market for clinicians and healthcare organizations seeking to modernize clinical programs with RPM technologies. Thus, the following chapters will seek to lend some clarity to the overall knowledge surrounding RPM-inclusive virtual care models.

So do RPM programs actually improve health outcomes and patient satisfaction, and are they cost-effective?

AN EVIDENCE OVERVIEW

There are three groups of outcomes that are important when evaluating RPM programs for success. These items fall under the same areas of health-system improvement outlined by the Institute for Healthcare Improvement under the Triple Aim.[1]

First, it is important to understand the clinical benefits of the program itself compared to standard of care. Did the RPM program for patients with hypertension reduce their blood pressure? Did the weight-loss program reduce body mass index (BMI) or waist circumference? Did the program focused on diabetes management provide better blood glucose control? In summary, does the development of an RPM clinical model help patients achieve better health?

Second, the program should have benefits when it comes to controlling healthcare utilization and overall costs for a patient population. With better healthcare services like RPM, we should see improvements in terms of hospitalizations, emergency department visits, and other costly services that result from the poor management of chronic illness.

Third, it is necessary to understand the patient perspective of RPM programs. When done correctly, RPM programs provide a new experience with healthcare services, and with them come new challenges for patient engagement. For a program that is built along the principles of patient engagement, it is essential to understand patient satisfaction compared to standard clinical models. Do patients use the program long term? Do they express value? Are these models better than current face-to-face services?

RPM, as an area of focus for researchers, has grown substantially since 1997. I performed a keyword search in PubMed to see the trends in

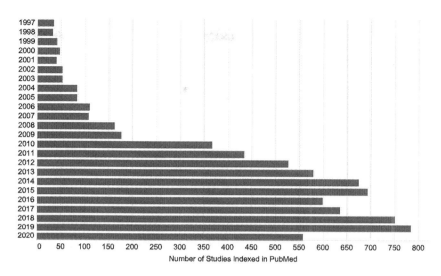

FIGURE 13.1
PubMed Results for Remote-Patient Monitoring.

publication over time related to RPM. Using the terms "remote," "patient," and "monitoring," I pulled the raw data and produced Figure 13.1. In 1997, there were fewer than 50 studies published, whereas, in 2019, there were close to 800 studies published covering the topic. After iPhones and smartphone ownership rates took off after 2007, the growth in RPM studies on PubMed accelerated.

Many people new to RPM models assume that this is a frontier area of healthcare services. While adoption has been slow in the market, the body of clinical evidence for these models is actually fairly robust, but somewhat lacking in definitional clarity.

Thus, I performed a literature review looking for systematic reviews and randomized clinical studies covering RPM models as well as studies that evaluate both the cost-effectiveness and patient perceptions of these clinical models.

Do RPM-Based Virtual Care Programs Work?

In 2016, a systematic review[2] reported findings on RPM programs across a wide range of chronic conditions and care settings. Sixty-two published studies were included in the review. Most of the studies looked at programs that incorporated a wide variety of interventions with multiple components, while a good portion of others looked at programs that primarily used a smartphone-based interface and some included wearables. This review is fairly comprehensive and provides good conclusions. By and large, the authors conclude that the majority of studies report positive findings with respect to health outcomes. According to this particular review, RPM-based virtual care programs improve health outcomes. But, it is more far complicated than that statement alone.

ECONOMIC OUTCOMES

One of the primary barriers to the widespread adoption of high-touch care models, more effective chronic disease management programs, and RPM-based virtual care programs is cost. High-touch and personalized models are costly when organizations operate on razor-thin FFS margins.

A systematic review[3] of economic evaluations performed by Peretz and colleagues looked at RPM program economics for older adults with chronic conditions. I specifically include this review because if these programs can be cost-effective for a higher-cost, higher-need population, then they will likely scale well into younger, less complex populations as well.

Thirteen studies were included in the review. The authors developed a new metric to compare across the studies called the combined intervention cost that included equipment purchases, servicing, and monitoring. They found that costs for the programs range from $275 to $7,963 USD annually.

The three primary findings from the study are as follows:

- Since 2004, RPM program costs have decreased due to lower-cost technologies.
- Monitoring a single vital sign is likely to be less costly than monitoring multiple vital signs.
- Programs focused on hypertension or CHF are less expensive than those focused on respiratory or multiple conditions.

Given these results, the value and ROI from RPM programs is then derived from reducing patient utilization of healthcare services and products. If this reduction is larger than the cost of operating the RPM-based virtual care program, then the program produces a positive ROI. The primary points of savings for RPM will likely be reductions in emergency department visits and hospitalizations from which avoided costs can far exceed the range reported from this study. Indeed, the following review of the evidence suggests that these outcomes are possible from programs, but further research is needed to understand the direct ROI attributed to RPM programs. As value-based payment continues to grow, it will be essential that RPM models pass the test of cost-effectiveness.

Patient Experience Outcomes

One of the primary benefits of virtual care programs is improvement in patient experience and satisfaction. More convenient and patient-centered program design frequently accompanies virtual care models, where healthcare services have traditionally lacked patient-centered design. Thus, it is important to understand the patient perspective of RPM-based models of care prior to and during implementation.

One systematic review[4] looked at 16 studies facilitated in eight different countries focused on understanding patient beliefs, attitudes, expectations, and experiences with RPM programs. The study included patients living with common chronic conditions such as COPD, heart failure, diabetes, hypertension, and end-stage kidney disease.

Four important outcome themes are important to understand from this review. Patients reported the following:

- Gained knowledge and improved positive health behaviors (i.e., cognitive and behavioral elements of patient engagement).
- Improved peace of mind and security from supportive monitoring (i.e., emotional elements of patient's engagement).
- Concerns about additional burden and work from monitoring.
- Fear about the loss of interpersonal connections and being confused by data (i.e., illustrating the importance of human involvement).

This review suggests that patients report gaining disease-specific knowledge, proactive identification of deterioration, improved ability to self-manage their disease, and greater ability to participate in shared decision-making. These are outcomes of significant importance to chronic disease management.

Patients in the study did express concerns that RPM would take away the personal connection to their physicians and the additional burden. It is important to note that this is an important reason that effective RPM programs have a strong level of clinician interaction rather than reliance on data collection alone. Patients still require and request a strong relationship with care providers despite the digitization of some care processes.

THE AHRQ SYSTEMATIC REVIEW

The most comprehensive review[5] of telehealth and virtual care models was conducted by the AHRQ by Totten and colleagues in 2016. They reviewed essentially all published systematic reviews on the topic to determine the effects of telehealth on clinical outcomes. For them, telehealth, the term, covered a wide variety of models that they effectively classified, defined, and separated to provide actionable information for healthcare decision-makers. This review is still a broad take on these models, as there is still a large number of variables that impact the performance of individual programs.

The researchers identified 1,494 publications about telehealth and found 58 systematic reviews that met the predesigned study criteria. Upon examining the reviews, the team mapped the evidence using visuals to describe the state of the evidence for these models. Figure 13.2 shows the categorization of the various models covered by the 58 systematic reviews.

RPM models, audio-visual telemedicine, and multifunction virtual care models make up 70% of the covered technology-enhanced care models. Virtual psychotherapy is also a significant portion of those models studied. Given the scale of this review, it provides excellent evidence as to which models or combinations of models show success in RPM and telehealth, generally.

Figure 13.3 shows the reviews mapped with respect to the number of patients in which the models were studied and the weighted benefit of the model on health outcomes. The shading of the bubbles indicates the number of studies reviewed in each bubble that include strength of evidence assessments. Thus, the "more SOE ratings," the higher likelihood that the outcomes reported are true.

The three most consistent, conclusive, and beneficial telehealth functions from this review indicate that models that use multiple functions

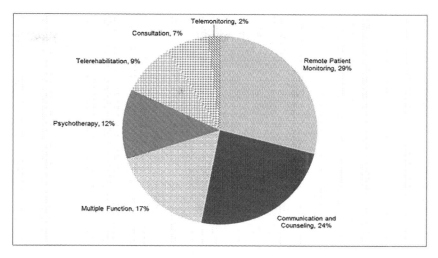

FIGURE 13.2
Distribution of Telehealth Functions Across Included Systematic Reviews.

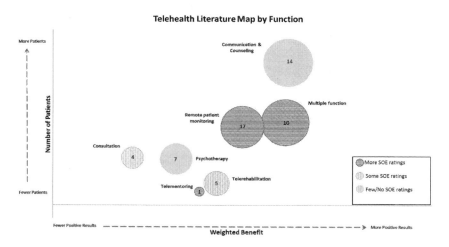

FIGURE 13.3
Telehealth Literature Map of Systematic Reviews by Modality.[6]

(i.e., coaching and RPM), RPM, and communication and counseling functions provide the most benefit to patients. In this case, RPM is RPM, and communication and counseling is the use of technology to facilitate the exchange of information between a patient and care team member designed to replace or supplement face-to-face care. The multiple functions category has aspects of both.

Indeed, the authors of the AHRQ review conclude with the following statement:

> The most consistent benefit has been reported when telehealth is used for communication and counseling or remote monitoring in chronic conditions such as cardiovascular and respiratory disease, with improvements in outcomes such as mortality, quality of life, and reductions in hospital admissions.

Out of the review comes the recommendation of the authors, that future research should focus on implementation and program best practices at the clinic level. This means more clearly defining program elements, costs, and activities that occur in these care delivery models as well as best practices in launching these programs.

It is important to mention that the systematic reviews covered by this AHRQ review are not indicative or representative of the scale and scope of various digital health-related clinical models in practice today, but rather this reflects the current state of the literature produced by researchers. Often, the market operates much faster than research can be generated, so the actual features of programs enrolling patients may differ from the categories described here.

NOTES

1. D. M. Berwick, T. W. Nolan, and J. Whittington. "The Triple Aim: Care, Health, and Cost." *Health Affairs*, 27(3) (2008 May/June): 759–769.
2. A. Vegesna, M. Tran, M. Angelaccio, and S. Arcona. "Remote Patient Monitoring via Non-Invasive Digital Technologies: A Systematic Review." *Telemedicine Journal and E Health,* 23(1) (2017): 3–17. https://doi.org/10.1089/tmj.2016.0051
3. D. Peretz, A. Arnaert, and N. N. Ponzoni. "Determining the Cost of Implementing and Operating a Remote Patient Monitoring Programme for the Elderly with Chronic Conditions: A Systematic Review of Economic Evaluations." *Journal of Telemedicine and Telecare,* 24(1) (2018): 13–21. https://doi.org/10.1177/1357633X16669239
4. R. C. Walker, A. Tong, K. Howard, and S. C. Palmer. "Patient Expectations and Experiences of Remote Monitoring for Chronic Diseases: Systematic Review and Thematic Synthesis of Qualitative Studies." *International Journal of Medical Informatics,* 124 (2019): 78–85. https://doi.org/10.1016/j.ijmedinf.2019.01.013

5. A. M. Totten, D. M. Womack, K. B. Eden, M. S. McDonagh, J. C. Griffin, S. Grusing, and W. R. Hersh. "Telehealth: Mapping the Evidence for Patient Outcomes from Systematic Reviews." Technical Brief No. 26. (Prepared by the Pacific Northwest Evidence-based Practice Center under Contract No. 290–2015–00009-I.) AHRQ Publication No.16-EHC034-EF. Rockville, MD: Agency for Healthcare Research and Quality; June 2016. Online. www.effectivehealthcare.ahrq.gov/reports/final.cfm.

6. Ibid.

14

Digging Deeper: RPM Outcomes by Condition

It is important to recognize not only that each patient is unique but that each RPM program and population under care may also be unique. Taking the approaches from a hypertension-focused RPM clinical program and applying them to an oncology program may not yield the same results, even if the physiological parameters being monitored are relevant.

Hypertension, and its negative effects, can be treated using a combination of dietary changes, pharmacologic interventions, improved activity, weight loss, reduced sodium intake, stress reduction, and a decrease in alcohol consumption. Whereas patients with cancer face a condition that is driven by a cellular or genetic abnormality that causes uncontrolled cell growth, a healthy diet, stress reduction, and improved activity may improve long-term or population outcomes, but the cancer itself likely will not be mitigated from robust lifestyle modifications alone.

Thus, it is important to understand the current state of the evidence for specific conditions or groups of conditions with respect to RPM-based programs.

**

I performed a literature review using PubMed to search for either systematic reviews or individual clinical programs that show efficacy or effectiveness across a number of common disease groups.

While there is sufficient positive evidence that suggests that RPM-centered models have positive effects on clinical outcomes, patient engagement, and sometimes even cost, each program is unique and results are not necessarily always generalizable. Execution, population studied, setting of care, technologies used, the specific care team members providing care, and conditions studied all have a big impact on how things turn out in clinical evaluations.

Figure 14.1 shows a map of the conditions of focus in the published studies included in the comprehensive ARHQ telehealth review. The x-axis shows the results of the studies with respect to the benefit to patients, and the y-axis plots the number of patients included in the conclusions as a surrogate for the robustness of the evidence.

This evidence map shows the state of our understanding of the benefits of telehealth models, broadly, by condition. The most positive results show benefit in mixed chronic conditions, while the most studied specific conditions are cardiovascular disease and diabetes, with behavioral health closely following. These telehealth, virtual, and RPM-based clinical models have been studied in a wide range of conditions and have demonstrated positive effects for patients. The following section of the book digs deeper into systematic reviews by condition to provide additional depth to the current state of knowledge.

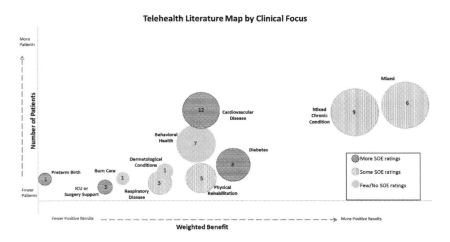

FIGURE 14.1
Telehealth Literature Map of Systematic Reviews by Clinical Focus.[1]

Improving Physical Activity and Diet

From the umbrella review,[2] *Telemedicine in the OECD*, the authors assessed four reviews of virtual care programs using RPM interventions to improve nutrition and physical activity—both important behavioral changes in chronic disease management and core areas of opportunity for digital health.

All four reviews found that these interventions were at least as effective as usual care. Equal performance to current standard of care is crucial to establish because it allows the other benefits of virtual care models to be the primary drivers of adoption (e.g., convenience, access, cost-effectiveness). However, the authors also note that the addition of RPM to a virtual program focused on lifestyle resulted in better outcomes with respect to increasing physical activity. This was concluded from studies directly comparing to face-to-face care seeking the same outcome.

Evidence from this systematic review also found that RPM combined with video/telephonic consultations can improve diet quality and fruit and vegetable intake among patients with chronic conditions. This review is by no means comprehensive, but the early evidence suggests that the idea that digital health technologies can allow healthcare services to more effectively impact individual behaviors.

Heart Disease and Diabetes: The Pioneer Conditions

Heart conditions and diabetes are the two conditions most studied with respect to RPM and virtual care. This is primarily due to the high prevalence, the well-defined treatment protocols, and the potential for lifestyle change to produce meaningful improvement in patient condition.

In a robust meta-analysis and systematic review[3] looking at 27 clinical trials, the authors found that mobile app (i.e., RPM)–assisted self-care interventions are effective tools for managing both hypertension and diabetes. The study found that both HbA1C levels and blood pressure outcomes were improved through the analysis across all 27 clinical studies examined.

The authors suggest that this is due to the personalized self-care recommendations provided to patients resulting from RPM data collection. They suggest that the combination of data collection and more effective communication with the patient drive the clinical benefit. Equipping patients with their own data as well as behavioral recommendations based on it is an example of clinical programs engaging with patients on cognitive and behavioral levels. The results show that the following program elements produce benefit: self-management, health data visualization, medication monitoring, frequent communication with healthcare providers, app-delivered automated feedback, personalized health goal setting, various forms of reminders, and the provision of education materials.

Diabetes and hypertension are two highly prevalent and impactful chronic conditions around the world. Innovations that can improve the management of these conditions are crucial to the future of healthcare services. This study has a large sample and provides some robust and conclusive evidence that these hybrid virtual care and RPM programs are effective.

A Diabetes Case Study

In the United States, type 2 diabetes is a major chronic disease. CDC data[4] in 2020 shows that over one in ten, or 34.2 million, Americans has diabetes. This number is increasing, as indicated by the number of Americans with prediabetes, which is one in three, or 88 million people.[5] This represents a major area of opportunity for the use of digital health technologies.

An RPM-based model using connected devices plus real-time health coaching is proving to be the most effective for diabetes. One study[6] looked at the use of two-way messaging glucose meters with access to certified diabetes educators. The randomized clinical trial enrolled 330 adults with type 2 diabetes with an HbA1C > 7.5 and a BMI > 25 kg/m^2.

Patients were enrolled into four study groups to assess the specific program features that produce the most patient benefit. One group was the control, where they received no further intervention. One group received a connected scale in addition to their glucose meter. One group received the scale and low-intensity health coaching, and another group received the same with high-intensity health coaching. The study ran for 12 weeks.

The study found that the connected blood glucose meter alone improved blood glucose control as measured by HbA1C reduction. Importantly, the addition of health coaching resulted in even better results, with the higher-intensity coaching group showing the highest level of improvement in both weight loss and blood glucose control.

The evidence from the AHRQ review as well as the program evidence from Dr. Weidner and Angie's work suggests that this connected-care model that leverages human coaches and digital engagement platforms for RPM will become the dominant model of virtual care.

Heart Failure

CHF is another condition that receives a good deal of attention in RPM and virtual care research due to its prevalence and high spending. Heart failure is the 27th most costly ($33.4 billion) condition annually in the US.[7] CHF is also a condition of major relevance to health systems and hospitals due to the high rates of readmission for patients discharged with a CHF diagnosis. Fortunately, the evidence suggests that RPM programs can significantly improve outcomes for patients with CHF.

To assess the effectiveness of RPM programs designed for CHF, Bashi and colleagues conducted a systematic review[8] of systematic reviews. They identified 19 such reviews for consideration in their analysis. The review found substantial evidence that RPM-based virtual care programs and home telehealth are effective in reducing heart failure rehospitalization and mortality.

Neurological Disorders

Hypertension, diabetes, and CHF have been the core focus of most research on RPM. However, neurological disorders like Parkinson's disease and dementia are also high-impact chronic illnesses that require adequate management and high-touch clinical models. They also contribute to significant healthcare costs globally and are growing in prevalence with an aging population in many developed countries. In the US, dementias are the condition with the ninth most attributed healthcare spending annually at $79.2 billion.[9]

A systematic review[10] of the use of RPM in neurological disorders looked at 137 studies that span a number of diseases. Sixty-one studies covered in the review looked at multiple sclerosis; 41 focused on stroke; 20 looked at Parkinson's disease; 11 looked at dementia; 2 looked at traumatic brain injury; and 1 at ataxia.

While blood pressure and blood glucose are overt metrics of the diseases in hypertension and diabetes, neurological conditions can be monitored using a variety of metrics such as physical activity, range of motion, activity of daily living tracking, and limb functionality. The monitoring of patients with dementia or Parkinson's disease can also help prevent falls, which lead to further complications, healthcare spending, and even death (see Chapter 10).

This systematic review suggests that RPM is possible across a variety of neurological diseases and inpatient populations with a wide range of condition severity and disability. Wearables are accurately able to measure and monitor physical activity.

COPD

COPD is in the top 30 highest-cost conditions in the United States.[11] A systematic review[12] by Baroi et al. evaluated 15 studies looking at remote-respiratory assessments and their impact on health outcomes.

The study reports that most metrics in COPD-focused RPM programs involve the collection of forced expiratory volume using a spirometer, while others looked at resting respiratory rate, respiratory sounds, and end-tidal carbon dioxide level.

Patients report a high level of satisfaction from these programs, and studies suggest benefits to health outcomes, according to the authors. Specifically, these metrics allow for the early identification of condition exacerbations leading to possible prevention of costly episodes of care or patient injury. Organizationally, the authors indicate that these programs are feasible when combined with sufficient clinical staff and organizational support. Given the growth and affordability of connected medical devices like inhalers, spirometers, respiratory rate monitors, and pulse oximeters, RPM programs for COPD are not only possible but also accessible.

Asthma

Asthma is also in the top 30 highest-cost conditions in the United States.[13] As of 2018, according to CDC asthma prevalence data, approximately 24 million Americans have asthma. Approaches to asthma management primarily revolve around the management of attack trigger exposures, adherence to inhaled corticosteroids, and availability of rescue inhalers. Companies like Propeller Health have built a smart inhaler and mobile application to help patients both manage triggers and track their adherence, while feeding that data to the patients care team for RPM-based programs.

This type of program may be particularly helpful for younger patients with asthma, with whom emergency department visits related to asthma are common. Evidence[14] from one meta-analysis suggests that effective asthma education and action plan development can reduce emergency department visits and hospitalizations. Action plans and education built in a mobile application can be more engaging for younger patients, but when built with RPM in mind, they can also allow patients to track their progress with respect to that action plan.

Two systematic reviews have assessed the effectiveness of RPM models for the treatment of asthma. The first review found that mobile app–based RPM interventions with clinician support improved asthma control and reduced exacerbation rates.[15] Another separate review concluded that RPM interventions had small beneficial effects on asthma control.[16] The success of companies like Propeller Health and the results from these reviews suggest that these models are effective and acceptable to patients.

Oncology

My mom did not receive RPM during her care. As her caregivers, we collected of a wide variety of physiological metrics like blood pressure, weight, heart rate, respiratory rate, and physical activity, but we did not transmit these in real time to her care team. The only interactions we had with the care team was if we called for an emergency or showed up to the emergency department or during face-to-face visits in the clinic to which we brought our pink binder of metrics on paper—that were never actually reviewed because it would take too long for a provider to comb through the pages of the binder. However, there is growing interest, due to the success of RPM models in other conditions, in exploring how virtual care models can support oncology patients.

Oncology represents a more difficult RPM population due to the fact that the direct metrics of the disease are not measurable in the home by medical devices—they are most often imaging or laboratory diagnostic test–based. However, patients receiving treatment for cancer often develop significant monitorable conditions as a result of treatment or the condition itself.

My mom's leukemia, for example, was monitored via bone marrow biopsy procedures and polymerase-chain reaction lab tests—not really possible to conduct in the home. However, during treatment, she developed CHF, blood glucose control issues, physical disability and experienced significant pain. These conditions are highly monitorable in RPM programs to detect potential decompensations resulting from these comorbidities. Patients with cancer also experience significant mental health ramifications and fear; thus, RPM and telehealth programs have shown an ability to provide reassurance and a reduction in treatment burden due to a high number of outpatient and inpatient visits.[17]

Due to the variability in patient comorbidities and individual cancers, RPM programs focused on oncologic conditions do not benefit from the higher level of uniformity and process standardization that is possible in hypertension, CHF, and diabetes programs. Two available systematic reviews provide an excellent overview of RPM and other telehealth-based models in oncology.

One review[18] of 77 publications across 41 health systems concludes with a positive outlook for the use of digital solutions in oncology. The authors suggest that the current early evidence supports the use of RPM and telehealth to support patients with side effect management and other patient-centered outcomes like comfort level, pain, and reduced treatment burden.

The authors suggest, just like I do, that their review illustrates the need for standardization of program elements due to the wide range of interventions and digital tools used in the studies included in the review. The use of these technologies will continue to move into oncology as success is seen in other disease groups. For patients with comorbidities that have established RPM-based virtual care models, the potential is there to incorporate into oncological care delivery models. Underscoring the potential in oncology, Memorial Sloan Kettering, a world-class cancer treatment institution, launched a technology innovation accelerator in 2020 with an emphasis on RPM and virtual care technologies.

Pediatrics

We know that younger people have the highest rates of smartphone ownership in the country, when segmenting by age group and therefore smartphone-based RPM-based care models have the potential for strong engagement and adoption in this age category. However, at large, younger people have a lower prevalence of chronic illness and therefore are not a major area of focus for RPM care models—asthma is a major concern for pediatric populations, so this is an area of early exploration. However, currently there is not enough evidence in pediatrics to draw sweeping conclusions.[19]

We do have good evidence, however, that app-based approaches to healthcare for young adults are acceptable and useful. I worked for one of the first medication management mHealth companies to develop an app on the market, Dosecast®. In a 2017 study[20] looking at the acceptability of this application in a population of young adults with cancer, the results were very positive. Roughly the entire study population used the application at least once, and greater than 50% indicated that they took their medications immediately when prompted via the app-reminder system. Importantly, the patients reported that the app was intuitive and useful for managing their condition.

A review[21] by Sasangohar and colleagues (2018) suggests the same conclusion, but that limited study conditions and small sample sizes of studies in pediatric populations do not allow for generalization about effectiveness yet. However, given the affinity for smartphones by younger people, it is conceivable that success in adult populations for specific conditions may transfer well into pediatric settings.

In the US healthcare market, the rise in risk-based contracting and value-based payment will drive more research into how digital health tools can better support children and adolescents in experiencing better health outcomes. Under FFS, payment for RPM is highly limited in Medicaid and commercial insurance markets under which the majority of children are covered. Thus, from a market perspective, there is currently little incentive for companies to target a pediatric population for RPM given the lack of payor reimbursement. The growth of value-based contracting in this space will open opportunities for the future.

Mental Health

Mental health assessment, monitoring, and treatment are highly subjective and do not overtly seem to mesh with the concept of RPM due to the perception of RPM as strictly "physiological monitoring." However, this area has been heavily studied with respect to the use of telehealth, telepsychiatry, and even more subjective RPM. Mood tracking, patient assessment tools, automated CBT, and physical activity tracking are common approaches using digital tools in mental healthcare.

The prevalence and cost of mental and behavioral disorders are extremely high, with annual spending around $180 billion,[22] making this category the seventh highest diagnostic grouping with respect to total healthcare spending. Depressive disorders, in particular, are the 13th highest[23] individual condition with respect to spending ($67.5 billion). Furthermore, these estimates are the direct spending attributable to these conditions—many persons with mental and behavioral illness experience other physical comorbidities exacerbated by or brought on by their mental health condition. Thus, the full economic footprint of mental and behavioral illness is likely much larger.

One of the primary reasons for the interest in digital health models in mental health is the lack of sufficient workforce to meet patient demand in many countries—especially the US. Digital tools can help improve the supply of mental health professionals to remote areas or in areas with high demand but limited supply of professionals in the immediate physical location. In addition, there is interest in extending the capacity of existing providers through the use of RPM and hybrid clinical models that leverage mobile applications. In particular, there are efforts[24] by digital health companies and healthcare organizations to fully automate some CBT standards of care to deliver by stand-alone apps in order to help patients with limited access to face-to-face services or human healthcare providers. There are a few digital therapeutic apps with FDA approval as treatments for specific behavioral health conditions.

A research mentor of mine, a psychologist at Georgetown University, and I conducted a rapid review[25] of the evidence for consumer-focused mental health apps with marketing claims that suggest effectiveness in depression, anxiety, and stress. The early evidence is overwhelmingly positive with respect to a reduction in symptoms for these conditions. However, further research and regulatory oversight is needed to ensure adequate consumer protection.

Similarly, one systematic review,[26] specifically looking at depression and bipolar disorder, examined nine clinical studies to evaluate the effect of remote-mood monitoring on patient health outcomes. The authors conclude that remote-mood monitoring was effective at improving depression scores but not mania scores. The interventions may be effective at improving symptoms of depression, treatment plan adherence, and the identification of potential adverse events.

Still, the approaches vary widely, as supported by one systematic review[27] of RPM, telehealth, and other technologically enhanced models of care for serious mental illness. The authors conclude that, in particular, RPM and telephonic technologies are effective for some outcomes like medication adherence. However, overall, there is not yet sufficient standardization and research to draw major conclusions on the effectiveness of RPM-based virtual care models in mental health conditions. Depression and anxiety currently have the strongest evidence for the efficacy of certain app-based interventions.

We do know that telemental health services using audio-visual technology is equal in effectiveness to face-to-face care, and the addition of mobile applications for mood tracking, automated CBT, patient education, and other interventions is showing promise.

Chronic Kidney Disease (CKD)

CKD is the 40th most expensive condition with respect to annual spending, at $19.7 billion.[28] According to the National Kidney Foundation, diabetes and hypertension are the two primary causes of CKD, accounting for two-thirds of the cases. Thus, RPM-based virtual care programs focused on diabetes and hypertension have the potential to reduce the incidence of CKD by more effectively managing those precursor conditions.

A systematic review[29] of eight randomized controlled trials looking at the effects of RPM in CKD was performed by He and colleagues. The study suggests that RPM-based CKD care programs can improve the quality of life for patients. With respect to economic outcomes, the study suggests that these programs can result in significant reductions in hospital readmission rates, emergency department visits, and inpatient days in the hospital. The authors also add that adherence to the programs using RPM tends to be high, suggesting good acceptability and satisfaction from patients.

Emerging Areas of Study

Given the success of RPM-based virtual care models in the early conditions studied and the growth of available evidence, there has been slow but continuous adoption of these models by care delivery organizations.

One review from Huang and colleagues from 2014 explored the use of RPM in the management of inflammatory bowel disease. The authors suggest that remote-monitoring interventions produced positive health and economic outcomes. Specifically, the programs studied reduced clinic visit utilization compared to face-to-face models and showed parity with face-to-face models with respect to relapse rates, inpatient admissions, and overall quality of life.[30] This suggests that there is interest in these models broadly and to treat specific conditions.

Importantly, as suggested by Dr. Weidner, the use of physician-extenders, clinical staff, and allied health professionals is important to the implementation of cost-effective RPM-based virtual care models. Evidence suggests that models relying on allied health professionals and nurses are as effective in the virtual environment as face-to-face care.[31] Indeed, high-touch models of care are often seen as impossible due to the limited capacity for face-to-face visit volume at brick-and-mortar locations and advanced healthcare provider capacity. Virtual models can increase capacity and effective routing to the appropriate level of care provider to allow for better scalability.

NOTES

1. A. M. Totten, D. M. Womack, K. B. Eden, M. S. McDonagh, J. C. Griffin, S. Grusing, and W. R. Hersh. "Telehealth: Mapping the Evidence for Patient Outcomes From Systematic Reviews." Technical Brief No. 26. (Prepared by the Pacific Northwest Evidence-based Practice Center under Contract No. 290–2015–00009-I.) AHRQ Publication No.16-EHC034-EF. Rockville, MD: Agency for Healthcare Research and Quality; June 2016. Online. www.effectivehealthcare.ahrq.gov/reports/final.cfm.

2. N. D. Eze, C. Mateus, and T. Cravo Oliveira Hashiguchi. "Telemedicine in the OECD: An Umbrella Review of Clinical and Cost-effectiveness, Patient Experience and Implementation." *PLoS ONE*, 15(8) (2020): e0237585. https://doi.org/10.1371/journal.pone.0237585

3. K. Liu, Z. Xie, and C. K. Or. "Effectiveness of Mobile App-Assisted Self-Care Interventions for Improving Patient Outcomes in Type 2 Diabetes and/or Hypertension: Systematic Review and Meta-Analysis of Randomized Controlled Trials [published correction appears in JMIR Mhealth Uhealth. 2020 Aug 19; 8(8): e23600]." *JMIR Mhealth Uhealth.* 8(8) (2020): e15779. Published 2020, August 4. https://doi.org/10.2196/15779

4. National Diabetes Statistics Report, 2020. Centers for Disease Control and Prevention.

5. Ibid., 124.

6. J. B. Bollyky, D. Bravata, J. Yang, M. Williamson, and J. Schneider. "Remote Lifestyle Coaching Plus a Connected Glucose Meter with Certified Diabetes Educator Support Improves Glucose and Weight Loss for People with Type 2 Diabetes." *Journal of Diabetes Research*, 2018 (2018): 3961730. https://doi.org/10.1155/2018/3961730

7. J. L. Dieleman, J. Cao, A. Chapin, et al. "US Health Care Spending by Payer and Health Condition, 1996–2016." *JAMA,* 323(9) (2020): 863–884. https://doi.org/10.1001/jama.2020.0734

8. N. Bashi, M. Karunanithi, F. Fatehi, H. Ding, and D. Walters. "Remote Monitoring of Patients With Heart Failure: An Overview of Systematic Reviews." *Journal of Medical Internet Research*, 19(1) (2017): e18. Published 2017, January 20. https://doi.org/10.2196/jmir.6571

9. J. L. Dieleman, J. Cao, A. Chapin, et al. "US Health Care Spending by Payer and Health Condition, 1996–2016." *JAMA,* 323(9) (2020): 863–884. https://doi.org/10.1001/jama.2020.0734

10. V. A. Block, E. Pitsch, P. Tahir, B. A. Cree, D. D. Allen, and J. M. Gelfand. "Remote Physical Activity Monitoring in Neurological Disease: A Systematic Review." *PLoS ONE*, 11(4) (2016): e0154335. Published 2016, April 28. https://doi.org/10.1371/journal.pone.0154335

11. J. L. Dieleman, J. Cao, A. Chapin, et al. "US Health Care Spending by Payer and Health Condition, 1996–2016." *JAMA,* 323(9) (2020): 863–884. https://doi.org/10.1001/jama.2020.0734

12. S. Baroi, R. J. McNamara, D. K. McKenzie, S. Gandevia, and M. A. Brodie. "Advances in Remote Respiratory Assessments for People with Chronic Obstructive Pulmonary Disease: A Systematic Review." *Telemedicine and E Health Journal,* 24(6) (2018): 415–424. https://doi.org/10.1089/tmj.2017.0160

13. Ibid., 92.

14. J. M. Coffman, M. D. Cabana, H. A. Halpin, and E. H. Yelin. "Effects of Asthma Education on Children's Use of Acute Care Services: A Meta-analysis." *Pediatrics,* 121(3) (2008): 575–586. https://doi.org/10.1542/peds.2007-0113

15. C. Y. Hui, R. Walton, B. McKinstry, T. Jackson, R. Parker, and H. Pinnock. "The Use of Mobile Applications to Support Self-management for People with Asthma: A Systematic Review of Controlled Studies to Identify Features Associated with Clinical Effectiveness and Adherence." *Journal of the American Medical Informatics Association*, 24 (2017): 619–632. https://doi.org/10.1093/jamia/ocw143.

16. G. McLean, E. Murray, R. Band, K. R. Moffat, P. Hanlon, A. Bruton, et al. "Interactive Digital Interventions to Promote Self-management in Adults with Asthma: Systematic Review and Meta-analysis." *BMC Pulmonary Medicine*, 16 (2016): 83. pmid:27215329

17. A. Cox, G. Lucas, A. Marcu, et al. "Cancer Survivors' Experience With Telehealth: A Systematic Review and Thematic Synthesis." *Journal of Medical Internet Research*, 19(1) (2017): e11. Published 2017, January 9. https://doi.org/10.2196/jmir.6575

18. L. Warrington, K. Absolom, M. Conner, et al. "Electronic Systems for Patients to Report and Manage Side Effects of Cancer Treatment: Systematic Review." *Journal of Medical Internet Research,* 21(1) (2019): e10875. Published 2019, January 24. https://doi.org/10.2196/10875

19. It is also never really possible to draw sweeping conclusions here because of the lack of generalizability of clinical models among settings, providers, conditions, and patient populations.

20. Y. P. Wu, L. A. Linder, P. Kanokvimankul, B. Fowler, B. G. Parsons, C. F. Macpherson, and R. H. Johnson. "Use of a Smartphone Application for Prompting Oral Medication Adherence Among Adolescents and Young Adults With Cancer." *Oncology Nursing Forum*, 45(1) (2018): 69–76. https://doi.org/10.1188/18. ONF.69-76

21. F. Sasangohar, E. Davis, B. A. Kash, and S. R. Shah. "Remote Patient Monitoring and Telemedicine in Neonatal and Pediatric Settings: Scoping Literature Review." *Journal of Medical Internet Research*, 20(12) (2018): e295. Published 2018, December 20. https://doi.org/10.2196/jmir.9403

22. J. L. Dieleman, J. Cao, A. Chapin, et al. "US Health Care Spending by Payer and Health Condition, 1996–2016." *JAMA,* 323(9) (2020): 863–884. https://doi. org/10.1001/jama.2020.0734

23. Ibid., 100.

24. Longyear, R. L., and Kushlev, K. "Can Mental Health Apps Be Effective for Depression, Anxiety, and Stress During a Pandemic?" *Practice Innovations*, (2021). Advance Online Publication. https://doi.org/10.1037/pri0000142

25. Ibid.

26. A. S. J. van der Watt, W. Odendaal, K. Louw, and S. Seedat. "Distant Mood Monitoring for Depressive and Bipolar Disorders: A Systematic Review." *BMC Psychiatry*, 20(1) (2020): 383. Published 2020, July 22. https://doi.org/10.1186/ s12888-020-02782-y

27. S. Lawes-Wickwar, H. McBain, and K. Mulligan. "Application and Effectiveness of Telehealth to Support Severe Mental Illness Management: Systematic Review." *JMIR Mental Health,* 5(4) (2018): e62. Published 2018, November 21. https://doi. org/10.2196/mental.8816

28. Ibid., 100.

29. T. He, X. Liu, Y. Li, Q. Wu, M. Liu, and H. Yuan. "Remote Home Management for Chronic Kidney Disease: A Systematic Review." *Journal of Telemedicine Telecare,* 23(1) (2017): 3–13. https://doi.org/10.1177/1357633X15626855

30. V. W. Huang, K. M. Reich, and R. N. Fedorak. "Distance Management of Inflammatory Bowel Disease: Systematic Review and Meta-analysis." *World Journal of Gastroenterol,* 20 (2014): 829–842. pmid:24574756

31. R. Speyer, D. Denman, S. Wilkes-Gillan, Y-W. Chen, H. Bogaardt, J-H. Kim, et al. "Effects of Telehealth by Allied Health Professionals and Nurses in Rural and Remote Areas: A Systematic Review and Meta-analysis." *Journal of Rehabilitation Medicine,* 50 (2018): 225–235. pmid:29257195

15

Payment and Policy

Healthcare is arguably the most regulated industry in most countries around the globe. Aside from nuclear power plants, dangerous chemical manufacturing, and weapons, the imperative for healthcare organizations is to operate as safely as possible where human lives are on the line. Thus, organizations and individuals operating in healthcare maneuver in a box created by both systemic incentives and regulatory limitations.

Regulation in the US is shared across a number of government agencies: the FDA, which regulates pharmaceutical products and medical devices (e.g., wearables and RPM devices); CMS (e.g., coverage for services and reimbursement policy); state Medicaid Agencies (e.g., Medicaid program rules); the U.S. Department of Health and Human Services; and other key government entities.

In conjunction, the financing of healthcare is accomplished through a number of different markets. According to Kaiser Family Foundation research,[1] in 2018, 49% of the country was covered by employer-sponsored commercial insurance. Six percent of the U.S. population was covered by commercial non-employer insurance. Twenty percent of the country's people were covered by Medicaid, a federal–state partnership program, and 14% were covered by Medicare, a federal program. The military covers 1% of the population. Nine percent were uninsured.[2] These trends fluctuate over time, but at any given time, a government program funds greater than a third of the population in the US.

Across the variety of payors, there are different incentives and payment models utilized. Healthcare innovation and new technologies must operate and exist within the regulatory frameworks and funding sources defined by government, nonprofit, and commercial entities. While there are many motivators, financial incentives provide the most power when it comes to shifting the behavior of healthcare organizations and individual providers of healthcare services toward new clinical models. Payment incentives are the primary drivers of the adoption of new models of care and new technologies.

There are two dominant models of payment that affect the development and sustainability of virtual care models, in particular. FFS payment is the dominant model of payment in US healthcare, while value-based payment is a growing trend in the market. FFS is an excellent tool to incentivize and disincentivize certain health services at an individual service level. Value-based payment comes in many forms, but the most radical model in the current system is the full-risk model (e.g., ChenMed's payment model). In the current reimbursement and payment environment, both systems are currently incentivizing the adoption of virtual care and digital health technologies.

FFS PAYMENT MODELS IN VIRTUAL CARE

Payment models are a distinct function from the issue of insurance coverage. Determining health coverage eligibility and deciding who pays for the coverage is a separate issue dealt with in policy. Once coverage is obtained by an individual, the ways in which the money flows to the providers of services or products provided to that individual is the realm of payment models. These payment models in turn produce the financial incentives or disincentives for healthcare provider organizations.

In the United States, the FFS payment system is one of the tools used as a carrot rather than a stick. FFS payment models are, at a basic level, individual rates of payment per defined service provided to a patient. Simplistically, each time a physician or other healthcare provider performs a specified service tied to a billing code, that service is reimbursed at a predefined rate. The availability of billing codes, in this case, actually can dictate the mix of services rendered to patients rather than the other way around.

In the early days of telemedicine, obtaining FFS payment for services delivered via audio-visual technology was a major win. However, both the regulatory limitations and payment rates attributed to early telemedicine services hindered larger-scale adoption. There were strict rules for the setting of care established for the early days of telemedicine by a variety of payors. Often, only certain geographies were eligible (e.g., rural) for telemedicine services, and those services were sometimes required to be offered at a physical site rather than in the home of the patient. Over the years, various payors adopted new regulations for the provision of audio-visual telemedicine services.

Payment for telemedicine services was also historically held at a rate below that of in-person healthcare services, meaning that the same clinical processes carried out at a face-to-face visit were reimbursed at a higher rate than those offered via audio-visual technology. The goal for telemedicine advocates for many years was to remove the regulatory limitations and to achieve payment parity between in-person and telemedicine services.

The regulatory barriers and lack of payment parity drove much of the adoption and organizational behavior associated with offering early virtual care services to patients—even if those services allow for improved access to care, outcomes, or patient satisfaction. In the end, the power of the dollar in healthcare trumps all innovation efforts. If a new clinical model is not sustainable financially, then it will not last long or scale. Under FFS, this is the reality when it comes to innovation and the development of new virtual care delivery models.

But, FFS payment does have the unique benefit of incentivizing individuals' services by elevating the reimbursement rate for the desired services. For new services like RPM, which launched out of CMS in 2018, the payment rates can actually incentivize healthcare service providers to adopt the model. In fact, CMS has implemented some favorable reimbursement programs and rates to encourage organizations to begin offering services to patients with chronic illness during the transitions of care and in the home for this reason.

With respect to virtual care, CMS rolled out FFS payment requirements and rates for chronic care management (CCM) services, principal care management (PCM), transitional care management (TCM) services, and RPM as well as maintaining the reimbursement for traditional audio-visual telemedicine services.

The CCM, PCM, TCM, and RPM codes are an example of how FFS can be utilized to incentivize the adoption of new models of healthcare services for patients with chronic illness during the transitions of care or when the patient is not physically inside the four walls of the healthcare facility. While each has unique billing rules, requirements, and rates, each of them is designed with the goal of providing more proactive care services to patients with chronic illness.

With payment available, organizations offering healthcare services now have a clear funding stream from Medicare for eligible patients, some state Medicaid agencies, and sometimes from commercial payors. The basic services under these codes are designed to be performed using telephone communication, in person, and via email by unsophisticated programs, but digital health technologies allow more sophisticated programs to achieve better financial efficiency and engagement from patients.

The requirements set forth to bill these codes involve operational changes, patient communication, clinical data collection, and documentation needs that are well supported by digital technologies. The implementation of virtual care programs requires workforce augmentation, new training, brand new clinical workflows, and significant investment. The use of software and mobile applications to improve the cost effectiveness and efficiency of these programs is essential to their sustainability and effectiveness.

Importantly, each of these programs also requires a certain level of engagement from patients. Thus, the use of technologies to improve convenience, patient experience, and communication is arguably a cornerstone of programs taking advantage of these funding streams. Smartphones provide an excellent way to engage patients in their care by providing them with data and educational materials and to facilitate communication with care teams operating under a program developed through CCM, PCM, TCM, or RPM payment incentives.

These codes represent a FFS approach to incentivizing *high-value interventions*. Value is a term thrown around a lot in modern healthcare discussion, with a wide range of definitions and ideas. The idea, though, is to pay for or incentivize services that lead to better health outcomes and lower cost rather than services that are costly and have limited benefit to patients.

This line of thinking also coincides with the concept of *prevention*. The old adage suggests that an ounce of prevention is better than a pound of cure. Services like CCM, PCM, TCM, and RPM were implemented in order to pay for proactive services for patients with chronic illness in an attempt to improve the performance of the delivery of care to this important patient population. The funding streams set up allow for more time to be spent with patients at favorable rates for providers. Thus, the goal is to prevent mismanagement of chronic illness leading to emergency department visits, hospitalizations, and preventable specialty care.

FFS payment models, however, are problematic and even dangerous when applied to all services. While a useful tool for promoting high-value services, the inherent incentives also contribute to bad outcomes and reactive rather than preventive healthcare. In an FFS payment model, healthcare organizations are also incentivized to fill hospital beds, to perform as many services as possible, and to drive high patient visit volumes. When speed and volume are the incentive, the total cost of care for a patient or population increases as organizations seek to bill as much as possible. The speed incentives can also lead to "bare minimum programs." Under FFS, efficiency is needed for sustainability. Organizations seek to minimize cost and maximize revenue when each service is tied to a specific rate. So, the quality of the services may suffer when operations are focused on meeting only the minimum requirements to bill a code.

For example, RPM code billing requirements outline 20 minutes of clinical time spent on each patient each month. The activities and interventions performed during that 20-minute period can vary widely from wasteful time spent to high-touch models of patient engagement. A nurse assigned to perform RPM services could spend 20 minutes doing activities of limited value to the patient or that same nurse could engage in effective health coaching activities that incorporate RPM data into a larger virtual care clinical program like Dr. Weidner's and Angie Stevens's care model.

The FFS system has the potential to fund both important preventive services that utilize powerful digital technologies and high-volume, low-value services. Either way, these new reimbursement programs funded by CMS have set the stage for organizations to meaningfully adopt virtual care models using digital health technologies.

In other countries, like the UK or Canada, single-payor government healthcare coverage removes the limitations of FFS and allows for flexible investment in high-value services. These countries have a health system with aligned incentives to collectively reduce the total cost of healthcare services and to provide models of care that more successfully manage chronic illness. The UK system, for example, places a high level of importance on primary care services where models like CCM, TCM, PCM, and RPM are inherently incentivized if they offer benefit to patients.

VALUE-BASED PAYMENT IN VIRTUAL CARE

Value-based payment models exist on a continuum from FFS to full-risk models. There are many approaches and terminologies used in this emerging space, but the goal of any of them is to alter the behavior of healthcare provider organizations to push them to focus on cost-effectiveness and health outcomes.

| Fee-for-
Service | Pay-for-
Quality | ACO
Upside
Risk | ACO
Downside
Risk | Full-risk
Models |

The full-risk model of value-based payment provides practices and healthcare organizations with a per-patient per-month payment to manage the full-range of services for patients. Thus, with a sustainable set revenue per patient and financial incentives to reduce cost per patients, these provider organizations can focus on building clinical models that keep patients out of the emergency department and keep chronic illnesses under better management.

The optimal future for virtual care models is one where primary care is funded through full-risk approaches. This approach is favorable for virtual care for three reasons. First, the incentives for healthcare providers to provide high-value care services, like certain virtual care models, to patients are as strong as possible. Second, there are minimized limitations on providers due to the removal of the coding and billing system. Third, virtual care models can enable more cost-efficient operations that reduce overhead for full-risk providers. For example, a full-risk clinic could reduce office space by having providers work from home to see patients virtually.

Organizations like ChenMed are currently reaping the benefits of a full-risk value-based payment approach and demonstrating patient benefit at the same time. Under a full-risk model, clinics have the cash on hand to invest in clinical programs and technologies that yield ROI in patient outcomes and total cost of care.

Full-risk payment models ask organizations to actually improve the health of the populations they serve—or face adverse financial impact.

This is where technology has the ability to enable the delivery of efficient and engaging clinical programs.

If you ask an FFS healthcare provider about why their patients end up with poorly managed chronic conditions, in the emergency room, or hospitalized, they will likely say something like the following:

> I can't control their behavior. Once they leave my office, it is on them to follow my recommendations.
>
> **—An FFS trained physician**

> I see this patient once a year. I cannot control what happens outside my office and for the last year. Their HbA1C was fine last year, but now it is in the higher range. I don't know until they come back.
>
> **—An FFS trained healthcare provider**

These comments plague healthcare services and reflect the insight from Chapter 4 that traditional medical services have a limited impact on health outcomes for patients. Effective care delivery models are able to stretch traditional health services into individual behavior factors and socioeconomic factors, but these models require sufficient time, resources, and technologies to operate at scale—perfectly provided by full-risk payment models.

Full-risk organizations, with cash on hand, can better tailor services to patients by providing needed items and extra services. Unlike the common comments illustrated earlier, full-risk physicians do have the resources to reach into the home when patients are not physically located in their office. They also have the time to spend with each patient to promote positive behavior change, unlike under FFS where time, quite literally, is money.

CASE STUDY: CHENMED AND VIRTUAL CARE DURING THE COVID-19 PANDEMIC

During the early days of the Covid-19 pandemic, the leaders at ChenMed quickly recognized that they had a problem: their high-touch, in-person model of care could put their older patient population at risk of infection.

ChenMed is a full-risk primary care organization that cares for the highest-complexity, highest-cost demographic in the country—the frail, older adult population. This patient profile is also at the highest risk of severe complications or mortality from Covid-19.[3]

Under non-pandemic circumstances, ChenMed has demonstrated the effectiveness of their high-touch, full-risk model of care. According to Dr. Syed, the secret lies in their restoration of the doctor–patient relationship. ChenMed physicians spend more time (189 minutes versus 21 minutes) per year with patients than the national average[4] at more appointments[5] (8.3 versus 1.2 per year). During this extra time, providers can work with their patients to address social needs, to encourage positive health behavior change, and to identify higher-risk patients before they end up in the hospital. Patients also receive a weekly phone call from ChenMed to check-in. This model that prioritizes connection between the care team and patients works well and can be supplemented with virtual elements.

ChenMed's model has demonstrated a significantly lower (33.6% lower) rate of emergency department visits per 1000 in a 65+ population than the 14-county averages in neighborhoods in which they operate. Figure 15.1 compares ChenMed's rates to similar providers in their local areas.

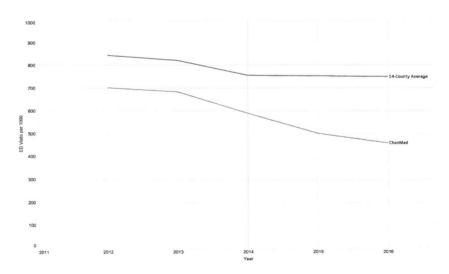

FIGURE 15.1
ChenMed ED Visits per 1,000 Compared to Similar Providers (65+ Population).

Along with anecdotal evidence from Dr. Syed, ChenMed's outcomes show the effectiveness of high-touch, connected primary care models. Patients benefit from this model in terms of health outcomes, cost of care, and satisfaction. Indeed, ChenMed reports[6] a Net Promoter Score of 92 in 2011. Top-tier scores in most industries are in the 70–85 range.[7]

During the Covid-19 pandemic, ChenMed rolled out a virtual care model to reach their patients via audio-visual telemedicine in addition to their weekly telephone calls to patients. Dr. Syed reports that even in a high-risk, older, and medically complex population, virtual care models were well received and ChenMed has plans to expand the program. Covid-19 accelerated ChenMed's digital strategy by a few years due to the success and scalability benefits of these models.

**

FFS and value-based payment models will always exist in the system as certain services require and benefit from FFS, while others, like primary care, are more effective if funded under a full-risk model. Bundling, capitating, and unbundling certain services each produce unique incentives for provider organizations, and thus careful effort must be taken to optimize each for specific conditions and services.

FFS offers virtual care programs the opportunity to generate new revenue streams, while value-based payment arrangements might push a clinic to implement virtual care models to generate cost savings and to improve quality metrics. The growth of virtual care has been fueled by Medicare FFS payments, but will find its cadence in full-risk payment models that need to effectively and efficiently provide services to patients. Importantly, virtual care can live well within all payment models.

NOTES

1. Kaiser Family Foundation estimates based on the Census Bureau's American Community Survey, 2008–2018.
2. It is honestly rather incredible that the uninsurance rates in the wealthiest country on earth are this high. In the end, when this group of people do not have access to preventive and primary care services, they end up getting sick and the country pays for it anyway through uncompensated care.
3. A. Garnier-Crussard, E. Forestier, T. Gilbert, and P. Krolak-Salmon. "Novel Coronavirus (COVID-19) Epidemic: What Are the Risks for Older Patients?" *Journal of the American Geriatrics Society*, 68(5): 939–940. https://doi.org/10.1111/jgs.16407

4. 2014 National Ambulatory Medical Care Survey; 2014 State and National Summary Tables; Table 30.

5. 2014 National Ambulatory Medical Care Survey; 2014 State and National Summary Tables; Tables 2 and 8.

6. Craig Tanio and Christopher Chen. "Innovations At Miami Practice Show Promise For Treating High-Risk Medicare Patients." *Health Affairs* (6) (2013): 1078–1082. https://doi.org/10.1377/hlthaff.2012.0201.

7. Satmetrix. 2011 net promoter industry benchmarks. San Mateo (CA): Satmetrix; 2011, February 27.

16

Digital Therapeutics

At the same time that telemedicine was getting started, the use of mobile apps grew rapidly. The advent of the iPhone lead to an explosion of opportunity for app developers to solve the problems of everyday and industry alike. To some extent, the decade of the 2010s can be marked as the app explosion. Following Apple's lead, Google quickly launched its Android operating system and developed partnerships with Apple's hardware competitors like Samsung.

As the app marketplaces became accessible to millions of people around the world, the technology developers began to develop applications that can leverage the powerful app store distribution channels. These marketplaces allow companies to quickly distribute new technologies to people around the world.

Naturally, the allure of such rapid distribution and the flexibility offered by mobile app software development has led to an explosion of interest in healthcare. Human health, it seems, is universal and still represents a frontier left to conquer along with outer space and the bottom of the oceans.

It did not take long for the apps to begin performing simple tasks related to health. The sharing of health information, medication interaction checkers, and pill reminder apps were on the scene fast. The early themes surrounded ways in which individual people can better remember items, check new information, and manage healthcare appointments. It was not until certain features, security, cloud technology, the internet, and wearable technologies expanded that RPM became widespread and possible. But, for the first time, in the late 2010s, a new topic began to explode—prescription digital therapeutics.

On June 15, 2020, the FDA approved the world's first prescription video game delivered on mobile devices, EndeavorRx (Akili Therapeutics). The digital therapeutic is a prescription-only game-based treatment for children (specifically, ages 8 to 12) with attention deficit hyperactivity disorder (ADHD). The therapeutic is indicated to improve attention function. While it is not a "cure," the treatment is designed to be included in a full program that can include in-person therapy, medication, and various educational programs to enhance patient attention outcomes.

In an FDA press release about the treatment, Jeffrey Shuren, MD, JD, director of the FDA's Center for Devices and Radiological Health, is quoted saying the following:

> The EndeavorRx device offers a non-drug option for improving symptoms associated with ADHD in children and is an important example of the growing field of digital therapy and digital therapeutics. The FDA is committed to providing regulatory pathways that enable patients timely access to safe and effective innovative digital therapeutics.

The era of digital therapeutics has arrived, and the science behind these new treatments is relatively new, but the evidence suggests that the interactions with the game or with features of other digital therapeutics can impact brain structures and activity.

While EndeavorRx is the first video game–based therapeutic, the first digital therapeutic, period, approved by the FDA, was reSET (Pear Therapeutics). reSET is indicated as a 12-week prescription-only treatment for patients with substance use disorder. The intended outcomes from patient use are increased abstinence from a patient's substances of abuse during the treatment program and improved patient retention in outpatient treatment programs. One of the primary patient characteristics required for a prescription is access to an Android or iOS tablet or smartphone—just like EndeavorRx and all digital therapeutics.

EndeavorRx's mechanism of action, according to Akili Therapeutics, is the delivery of sensory and motor stimuli to specific cognitive neural systems in the brain. The system is designed to directly generate physiological changes in the brain to improve certain cognitive functions. Similarly, Pear's reSET therapeutic is built to automate and digitize CBT principles to be delivered via smartphone. These are examples of two categories of approach in digital therapeutics, with some attempting to alter some body chemistry or physiological process and others attempting to support patient behavior change.

RPM versus Digital Therapeutics

Digital therapeutics are to pharmaceutical products what RPM programs are to in-person healthcare services. Both groups of technologies are a part of the digitization of healthcare through the widespread diffusion of the internet and smartphones. While the difference is subtle, there is a distinction between the two categories.

Digital therapeutics find their clinical footing through traditional pharmaceutical and medical device pathways. Companies prioritize clinical research up-front and the pursuit of US FDA market approval, European CE Marks, and Chinese National Medical Products Administration approval to begin selling in these markets.

RPM and virtual care programs tend, despite their technological base, to fall into the softer side of healthcare service interventions. They can address those high-impact areas of social and individual behavior risk factors while also enhancing the capabilities of medical services to become more proactive across a wide range of physiological, behavioral, and lifestyle metrics. The implementation of smartphone-based health data collection and more effective communication with healthcare providers of different clinical expertise is making traditional healthcare services more effective and engaging.

With digital therapeutics, some innovators have sought to remove the human clinician from the equation. The use of RPM enhances the effectiveness of clinical services and opens up new doors to experiment with clinical models, but it still requires healthcare providers and clinical staff to operate the programs. Digital therapeutics and the use of self-contained app-based interventions are gaining interest in healthcare to provide clinical interventions to patients using mobile devices and digital applications alone. Workforce availability issues, especially in mental health services, contribute to the desire for highly scalable and accessible app-based interventions.

Many digital therapeutic applications show early promise in terms of results, but continued research will be necessary to determine how they fit into the overall suite of clinical interventions available. As the industry moves forward in this space, it will be important to contextualize the self-contained technologies within the full clinical intervention tool kit. This means studying in larger patient populations in order to understand potential low-frequency adverse events, ensuring diverse study populations, and comparing outcomes to the current standard of care. It is essential that future studies include patient populations that are sufficiently diverse with respect to ethnicity, race, age, gender, geographic location, and incomes.

Due to the low-cost nature of many digital therapeutic applications, it is important to ask and answer these questions. Often studies that compare a digital technology directly to the standard of care do not happen because companies are afraid of a negative result. Comparing a new application versus a placebo or through the use of a wait-list control group has a higher likelihood of success. Some companies test the application as an "add-on" treatment where both study groups receive the standard of care, but one receives the mHealth application. Better understanding the places where these stand-alone apps add clinical and cost-effective value, however, will likely require the continued public funding of research and improved regulatory oversight.

17

Furthering the Field and Adoption

During my mom's inpatient stay while she battled leukemia, I spent hours that turned into days pacing around the hallways of the hospital. Those months and miles would prove an excellent teacher as we transitioned from multiple hospitalizations back to care in the home.

I learned a lot about how healthcare organizations operate and how they view the services they provide. But most importantly, I learned deeply about the patient experience, barriers, and needs across the continuum of care. I had the unfortunate opportunity to witness the full patient journey from chronic disease diagnosis through hospice care.

My belief in digital health technologies stems from the success of some of these models from an academic perspective due to their demonstrated outcomes, but the majority of my confidence comes from the experience of patient need. Patients need access to their health data, they need high-touch models of care, and they need support navigating their care journey. The use of efficient mobile technologies for data collection and communication just makes sense.

There are barriers to the widespread adoption of these models and technologies, but there are pathways that can be taken to break them down. Regulatory pressures and payment models are high-level barriers that have yet to catch up to the technologies and that require national coordination to achieve. Medical and healthcare education has not yet incorporated virtual care models and new patient engagement technologies into the curriculum. Organizations are still reeling from the failures of EHR implementation. Digital health companies market their solutions aggressively, creating confusion in the market among potential adopters. The diffusion of smartphones, wearables, and the internet has not yet reached

TABLE 17.1

Efforts to Overcome Virtual Care Model Adoption Barriers

• Invest in outcomes research	• Define effective program elements
• Refrain from drastic change claims	• Encourage a culture of experimentation
• Remain focused on patient engagement and experience	• Proactively prevent FWA
• Standardize terminologies	• Train clinicians to interact virtually
• Help push virtual care into curriculum	• Ensure alignment with payment models
• Help your older adult relatives learn to use virtual care	• Educate our legislators at national and state levels

all people, creating a potential equity issue.[1] And healthcare culture and organizational inertia within the system pose two of the highest barriers to overcome.

The "we have always done it this way" effect is exceptionally strong in healthcare. To combat this, those advocating for healthcare's digital future must work intentionally to advance the field by addressing the current barriers and through education.[2]

Innovators and leaders in digital health must do the following (see Table 17.1) to push the field forward in a manner that promotes sustainable change and that provides benefit for patients.

RESEARCH INVESTMENTS

Pharmaceutical and biotech companies spend approximately a billion dollars to bring a new drug to market.[3] Medication treatments fall under the "medical services" category of factors affecting health outcomes as they only address physiological processes that are involved in disease. Medications are an important part of modern healthcare services, but they alone are not enough to battle our chronic disease epidemic. If an organization or government wants to improve the health of their population, then a more holistic approach to health must be taken.

The numbers may not exist, but the among of money spent on R&D for new care delivery models, behavior change, social determinants of health, and patient engagement combined is likely far below that of pharmaceutical research R&D spending in 2019 (~$83 billion). Previously, there has been little financial upside for health services research investment outside of pharmaceutical products. With new risk-based payment models creating financial incentives, there is now an opportunity for financial upside driven by softer clinical models alone. Fortunately, as digital health companies and new technologies are brought to market, there will be a renewed interest and motivation for R&D in this area.

The current research shows positive outcomes in terms of health impact, cost-effectiveness, and patient satisfaction from certain virtual care models. We know that some of the top-performing programs have the capacity to significantly improve the treatment of many chronic illnesses that drive most healthcare spending across the globe.

The AHRQ review suggests that the evidence for RPM-based virtual care programs is sufficiently positive to merit adoption. But, as always, further research on individual technologies and specific programs is needed to develop a robust understanding of what works, for whom, in what settings, and for how long. Importantly, it is crucial to understand what specifically does not work. It is also essential to understand the factors that preclude a successful implementation of these programs at the organizational level as well as policy levers that can promote their widespread adoption and sustainability.

ENCOURAGING EXPERIMENTATION CULTURE

There has been a movement in recent years focused on creating *learning health systems*. The goal of this movement is to encourage a culture of continuous improvement and learning in healthcare delivery. Rather than accepting the current models of care delivery as the gold standard, learning health systems recognize that improvements can and should always be made. Thus, these organizations invest in internal research and development. The movement touches on the concept of encouraging a culture of experimentation in healthcare organizations.

With any new innovations, there are failures and lessons to be learned, but these should not discourage organizations and individuals from taking the steps toward something better. The adoption of an experimental mindset among healthcare providers and organizations can help facilitate meaningful steps toward the inclusion of new virtual care models into programs as well as the natural evolution of existing ones. Programs should solicit patient feedback, perform outcome evaluations, and seek to proactively improve models at frequent intervals. Dr. Weidner's experimental clinic used an agile methodology to iterate and build new clinical models without preconceived notions about how they should operate. It took experimentation and learning to achieve.

There is a collective fear of failure in healthcare due to the importance of the work, medical culture, and the human cost of errors. Healthcare organizations operate with their patients' lives and quality of their lives on the line. Thus, experimentation is often reserved for carefully controlled environments like academic medical centers and for clinical researchers trained in human subject protections. While clinical research has tremendous risks for patients, new interventions exist on a continuum from dangerous to fairly risk-free.

The beauty of many virtual care models is that they are simply enhancements to clinical models that already exist. This means that the risk to the patient is limited. Special care should always be taken to ensure human-subject protection, but experimentation with care delivery models using digital tools can be performed safely and done in partnership with patients. Dr. Weidner and Angie demonstrated the feasibility and success of doing this in their work.

When organizations adopt a patient-centered experimentation approach, risk is reduced and meaningful change can be made. Dr. Weidner and Angie made sure to include patients in developing their virtual care models proving that organizations can meaningfully partner with patients to work toward new, innovative models. Patients value this type of collaboration and benefit from it. This must be encouraged if virtual care models are to succeed.

PROGRAM AND TERMINOLOGY DEFINITIONS

One of the primary themes of this book is the illustration of the problems associated with terminology and definitions within the digital health industry. Throughout the book, the research presented uses certain terminology interchangeably and exclusively. Virtual care, telehealth, RPM, telemedicine, telemental health, connected care, health tech, mHealth, digital health, digital therapeutics, and other terms are used to describe many of the same technologies and care delivery models.

In order for the field to grow and new innovations to diffuse across healthcare service organizations successfully, the standardization of terminology and program elements must occur.

If I were a hospital administrator looking to develop my own virtual care service line, I would do the research on technologies and programs to identify the best practices in the space. Without adequate terminology standardization, I would be inundated with various technologies claiming different terms and functionalities that prevent me from comparing and identifying the best one for me. Once I have identified the technology, I will then have to select the level of clinicians to staff the solution, the specific interventions and clinical models to implement, and how to roll out to patients. Thus, in order to learn about the best practices in this space, I must review similar programs. Without standardization, it is difficult to identify elements that I can incorporate into my new virtual care service line.

When we write about these models, perform research, and market technologies, the terminologies must become standardized and program details must be outlined. Future systematic reviews must take special care to include only apples and not oranges.

PATIENT-CENTEREDNESS AND CLINICIAN TRAINING

Press Ganey is a consulting and research organization that provides a well-known patient satisfaction evaluation program. In 2020, they looked at patient satisfaction with telehealth services compared to in-person services.

Telehealth consultations already demonstrate a higher level of satisfaction among patients compared to in-person services (94.9% versus 92.5%).[4] However, as more healthcare organizations adopt virtual care models, the quality of clinician interactions with patients are likely to drive satisfaction and outcomes. Thus, for organizations seeking to implement, it is essential that virtual best practices are taught to clinical teams.

We learned from Dr. Faisel Syed, MD, that virtual care models can still be an intimate experience between a physician and patient—perhaps even more so than face-to-face care. The provider–patient relationship is still an essential part of evoking the emotional and behavioral aspects of patient engagement. The development of trust and the projection of clinical staff presence into the patient's home is a skill that must be instilled in care teams that provide care via these models. It is even more important in programs that seek to affect positive patient behavior change through connected and relationship-based virtual care for chronic illness. Relationships, though fostered virtually, are still an essential part of integrating technology into healthcare services. The development of "virtualist" training modules is essential to scaling programs at the healthcare organization level.

If the goal is to improve patient experience with health services and to affect patient health outcomes, then everything should be designed to impact patient engagement. Healthcare has been plagued by a lack of patient-centeredness since the beginning of the modern health system. But now, with efforts to better align payment incentives, organizations have the opportunity to entirely rethink their strategies, just like ChenMed. This will become increasingly important as new tech-enabled market entrants to healthcare begin to take market share away from traditional organizations due to a more patient-centric, or consumer-centric, healthcare offering. Training healthcare providers in maintaining best practice in virtual patient care supports this goal.

FWA

Since the early days of telemedicine, regulators and payors have been concerned about the potential for FWA. The physical healthcare visit requires more effort on behalf of the patient to attend; thus, there is a higher barrier to FWA when it comes to faking patient visits, though FWA still occurs.

But, with digitally delivered virtual care models, the potential to leave an electronic paper trail of documentation allows for bad actors to fake patient visits. The falsification of visit documentation or even RPM data is possible. Thus, payors and regulators fear that a lack of oversight and standardization in the industry could lead to the submission of billions of dollars in false claims or dollars lost to services rendered to patients with little medical value.

It is essential for the industry and those who implement these models to ensure compliance with payment policy and regulators. FWA concerns are a major barrier to widespread diffusion of these clinical models and must be addressed at all levels.

ENTRY TO CURRICULUM

In 2018, Dr. Lee H. Schwamm, MD, penned a letter[5] to the editors of *The Journal of the American Medical Association* (*JAMA*) arguing against the proposed development of a new medical specialty, the medical virtualist. He argues that this approach will risk furthering the divides in an already segmented and fragmented healthcare delivery system.

According to Schwamm, the rise of virtual care is a reflection of dissatisfaction with the unavailability of primary care or specialty care after hours or at unscheduled times. He is correct, but this reason is but a small facet of why virtual care is growing. The growth of digital across industries, the expectation of convenience by consumers, the desire to understand personal health data, the need for more effective communication, the ubiquity of smartphones, the unique cost-effectiveness of technology-enhanced programs, and the failure of current chronic disease models are also at play.

His suggested approach is not to create a new medical specialty, but rather to ensure that all clinicians are trained in the provision of effective virtual care. The view that a new specialty should be created is a traditional approach in medicine as new technologies are introduced to the market, but it is one that fails to build around the patient. Virtual care should not be viewed as a mutually exclusive service, but rather as a part of existing clinical programs. When built correctly, these programs act like a new service line complete with dedicated staff and operations, but from the patient's perspective they become cohesive parts of existing clinic operations. Thus, all clinicians and specialties will need to understand and implement virtual care models in their practice—or face significant competition and eventually loss of market share.

To achieve this goal, it is essential that both current and future clinicians gain exposure to and understanding of effective virtual care models for their area of focus. Digital health and virtual care advocates and researchers must support the inclusion of these technologies and models into healthcare and medical education.

DRASTIC CHANGE CLAIMS

"In-person services are a thing of the past" and "healthcare's future just went digital" are examples of headlines that make drastic change claims. These claims suggest that the current models of face-to-face care delivery will be entirely replaced with digital ones. This is an entirely possible outcome (aside from surgery and certain procedures) based on the results of other industries, but it will only occur gradually. However, what is more likely is a future of care delivery that involves a mix of virtual and in-person services.

Marketing materials and headlines from digital health companies try to set the stage for a future that leaves un-adapting organizations in the dust. Again, this future is within the realm of possibility as digital health models demonstrate better outcomes, cost-effectiveness, and patient satisfaction than traditional in-person services. Organizations that create better patient experiences and outcomes will dominate healthcare moving forward.

It is important, however, that leaders in the virtual care space recognize the resistance among many healthcare organizations to adopt models of care that are driven by technology. Healthcare's organizational inertia is a high barrier to overcome. To gain buy-in, innovators and advocates must stick to the evidence and point to a reasonable starting point for potential adopters. Digital transformation does not happen overnight, and aggressive tactics do not encourage meaningful collaboration toward the ultimate goal of better virtual care models for patients.

A journey of a thousand miles begins with a single step.

NOTES

1. Though the trends are positive and the Covid-19 pandemic has prompted significant investment in extending broadband internet connection and other technologies to rural communities.

2. This is why I wrote this book the way that I did.
3. O. J. Wouters, M. McKee, and J. Luyten. "Estimated Research and Development Investment Needed to Bring a New Medicine to Market, 2009–2018." *JAMA,* 323(9) (2020): 844–853. https://doi.org/10.1001/jama.2020.1166
4. A. Ramaswamy, M. Yu, S. Drangsholt, E. Ng, P. J. Culligan, P. N. Schlegel, J. C. Hu. "Patient Satisfaction With Telemedicine During the COVID-19 Pandemic: Retrospective Cohort Study." *Journal of Medical Internet Research,* 22(9) (2020): e20786. https://doi.org/10.2196/20786
5. L. H. Schwamm. "Virtual Care as a Specialty." *JAMA,* 319(24) (2018): 2559. https://doi.org/10.1001/jama.2018.5666

18

Our Moral Responsibility and a Compass

Change does not happen overnight, and the future of healthcare services is also not as black and white as marketing materials or futuristic predictions may suggest. Despite the inertia and the feeling that the mountains are immovable, healthcare organization leaders have the opportunity to define a new healthcare future.

I am guilty of idealism—and I admit this frequently. As a proud optimist, I like to believe that "good things" will eventually triumph over the status quo or "bad things." But, I am also a realist. I recognize and personally experience the tremendous barriers present in healthcare on a daily basis. However, I firmly maintain that it is not only essential but also a moral responsibility for healthcare professionals to seek continuous improvement in care delivery models and to implement new technologies when they demonstrate superiority.

Make no mistake, healthcare innovation and meaningful improvement to services is the pursuit of the moral good. This is part of what attracts many people to the healthcare industry as clinicians or otherwise. The opportunity to help patients and to live a life of purpose helping others is central to healthcare. Unfortunately, the burnout and barriers can cause people to lose sight of this incredible privilege. When the mission and the reality have diverged, it is time for a big revolution—and that is what we are seeing in healthcare currently.

Extending quality-life for people to spend with family, with friends, and in the pursuit of their own good is the moral good. When boiled down to a philosophical level, the improvement of health is the improvement of quality of life and the extension of quality time for people.[1] Regardless of individual circumstances and personal challenges, the extension of quality time to experience what it means to be uniquely human is a worthwhile pursuit. Life, the meaning of death, and life satisfaction are subjective to the patient, and thus the further personalization and expansion of healthcare services into new health-impacting factors is important to making our healthcare institutions better for all people.

I lost my mom during a particularly hot month of July in Atlanta when I was 20. In the years after that day, I struggled to accept and understand what happened. To some extent, I still grapple with the meaning of it all. I returned to school and continued to focus on studying the very system that caused so much struggle during a time where we had looked to it for hope and support. In the first year after, I was unable to do much more than study and try to keep moving forward.

During this period, I spent a good deal of time searching and yearning for the day I could look back on it all from a new perspective. For some reason, I knew that one day I would feel like I had overcome and accepted the trauma of it all. I knew that there would be a "reunion-show-esque moment" where I could view the whole thing from a different place and say, "Wow, that was a lot to handle."

Now, several more years later, I have realized that day will never come from looking back at what happened. The memories and stories will always be present, and those of us involved will all carry them with us for the rest of our lives—just as anyone who experiences loss in face of the healthcare system. What I have learned from this experience is that looking forward toward something better is the only way to find a place of comfort from the past. The respite that I have been searching for will only come from searching and advocating for something better for future patients.

I have always questioned the resistance that comes from healthcare professionals with respect to new innovations. As humans, we are all at risk of finding ourselves in a hospital bed or navigating a new care journey during our life. Indeed, the majority of us will find ourselves dependent on healthcare services toward the end of our lives. Why then, is there so much resistance to the new and a steadfast belief in the current models of care?

Folks, we all know that our current standard healthcare services leave patients adrift in a sea of uncertainty. Patients struggling with disease should not also struggle with navigating our systems. *It is not working.*[2]

A COMPASS

I was indoctrinated into Georgetown University's Jesuit Values during my time there. This is where I was introduced to the concept of *cura personalis*—which means, in Latin, care for the whole person. The concept calls for paying special attention to the personalized needs of individuals. This means recognizing each person's unique experiences, perspectives, values, and needs. All the work that I do in healthcare is driven by a firm belief in this value. The Jesuits developed this idea hundreds of years ago, prior to our scientific understanding of the factors that impact health outcomes. It is exceptionally interesting that the two belief systems arrived at the same conclusions about health—health science, too, supports the need for our models of care to become more holistic and personalized.

If you are reading this book, you might be a leader seeking to innovate in your healthcare organization. You might be late in your career looking to understand the new technologies and models coming down the road. You might be just starting off and looking to make your impact. You might be a student soaking up information and looking at new areas in which you can launch your career. You might be a leader in virtual care and digital health who continues to seek new ways of thinking and communicating your innovations. You might be an interested outsider with a vested interest in the quality of healthcare. Or, you might be a patient looking and hoping to find something better.

No matter your background, I offer the idea that *cura personalis* can be a guiding light for you in pursuit of better healthcare. When evaluating existing models of care, ask yourself whether they address important needs of patients—or better yet ask the patients. When seeking new models of care, ask the same. Does this new care model allow my care team to better understand the experience of the patient? Does my offering address social factors, individual behavior, physiological processes, and mental health factors? Am I helping patients engage with their health by supporting their cognitive, behavioral, and emotional experiences? Is this the care that I would like for myself or a loved one to receive? Am I offering a partnership with the patient along their care journey? Am I making life with a disease easier or am I adding to the burden?

These questions can be supplemented with objective scientific evaluation that explains how a new innovation might impact patient health outcomes, cost, and patient experience. *Cura personalis* combined with this scientific approach should guide your selection of new healthcare services. In fact, it should be your central guiding principle each day when you head off to work.

**

Innovation is a beautiful concept that has saved humanity from starvation, has extended life expectancies, and has improved the standard of living for billions of people from the beginning of known history. It is as human a pursuit as eating or sleeping. There have always been those among us who dream about a better future, those who seek to improve the status quo, and those who never take "no" for an answer.

Healthcare and medicine have always attracted, for the most part, people who wish to live a life of purpose helping others while facing tough intellectual challenges due to the complexity of health. I have seen, in recent years, a terrible amount of burnout and a collective loss of the beauty that attracts young people to the field.

The financial interest, volume-driven payment models, poorly designed information technology, regulatory barriers, inherent complexity, and a whole bunch of institutional inertia have stripped the human connection and effectiveness from healthcare services. As our institutions and healthcare organizations have grown in size and height, the connection to the patient has grown distant for many decision makers.

I have seen highly educated, passionate people lose their minds trying to make healthcare just a little bit better. They also lost their passion and belief in the idea that things can change for the better. Passion has been replaced by cynicism. They lost sight of the purpose of healthcare in the first place: to benefit both the individual patient and society as a whole.

Thus, we are sitting at a tipping point.

Fortunately, the growth of the smartphone and internet have opened new possibilities for those who seek to build a better healthcare future. Our path forward will involve the intentional implementation of new models of care for patients with chronic illness that result in the proactive pursuit of health. Change will come slowly as it always does, but we will blaze a new path forward by focusing closely on the needs of patients and following the evidence. All it takes is an open mind and a drive to build something better. With this, collaboration and leadership will guide our systems to a better future.

NOTES

1. The extension of life in absence of quality is not the same as the extension of quality life. Thus, I reject the common concept of "saving as many lives a possible" for this reason.
2. Let me be clear: virtual care is not the answer to all of healthcare's flaws. But I believe the use of technology can solve many of them.

19

Conclusion

There are two kinds of fools: one that says this is old and therefore good, and the other who says this is new and therefore better.

—William Ralph Inge

⁑

Around the same time I was writing this book, I was reading an incredible book edited by John Brockman. The book[1] is titled: *What Should We Be Worried About?* The work is a thought-provoking compilation of essays from some of our world's top scientists, authors, and professors. It is truly an esteemed group of thinkers.

The essays cover a wide range of topics across technology, climate change, nuclear disasters, political concerns, commentary on the general state of modernity, pandemics, the future of physics, and psychology—things that may not be of concern in the collective psyche but that are concerns of those who are deeply immersed in the subject matter.

One of the essays in particular caught my attention, and I immediately drew parallels to what I hope to convey about digital health and the continued development virtual care models. The essay, "The Contest Between Engineers and Druids" by Paul Saffo, discusses a societal phenomenon that I believe applies exceptionally well to the current state of technology acceleration and adoption in healthcare. Paul Saffo is a Silicon Valley-based forecaster who works on the long-term impact of technological innovation. He is an adjunct professor at Stanford's School of Engineering.

Saffo begins his essay with, "there are two kinds of fools: one that says this is old and therefore good, and the other who says this is new and therefore better." This serves as an introduction to the overall point comparing the group of people that are labeled the Engineers and another group referred to as the Druids.

The Druids, according to Saffo, are the group in society who argue that we must slow down and work to undo the disruptions and damage done by the rapid acceleration of technology since the beginning of the Industrial Revolution. Engineers are the opposite faction who argue that we can only produce better solutions to problems through the rigorous application of technological innovation. Engineers are the visionary futurists, whereas druids are the conservative traditionalists. Druids represent either a maintenance of the status quo or a complete reversion to the past.

Outside of healthcare, the tension between Druids and Engineers can be witnessed in areas like the creation of genetically modified organisms, gene therapy research, urban planning and, according to Saffo, anywhere where technology is applied to problems. In gene therapy, the Druids are concerned about the risks of editing genes and "playing-god" with the building blocks of life. The Engineers, obviously, see gene therapy as a powerful tool to combat disease and improve quality of life. In urban planning, the Druids might argue for de-urbanization and a return to local production, whereas the Engineers might suggest that artificial intelligence can make supply chains hyperefficient at bringing goods to distant urban centers. Druids might be a proponent for homesteading or home-based production of some goods and Engineers might support hyperspecialization to optimize productivity.

In healthcare, we have our own Druids and Engineers. The Druids are skeptical of technology and are strongly affected by the institutional inertia; in fact, they contribute to it. Healthcare's culture promotes a Druid-like mindset. The Druids, in this case, are the people who say, "this is the way we have always done things." The Engineers are innovators and visionaries who seek to apply technology to solve problems across the system from cost to health outcomes. The Engineers are fierce proponents of digital health and virtual care models, whereas the Druids may be skeptical and supportive of existing care models.

At this point, I am sure you believe that I am a proponent of the Engineer mindset. While I identify strongly with this group, I try to encourage people to adhere to an entirely different mindset from either of these. I believe that, given sufficient need, humans have the ability to use science and technology to address it. But, inflated expectations and quick decisions can also be detrimental when health is involved. The clinical vision for electronic health records was not realized due to rapid, poorly coordinated, forced adoption. Thus, while the Engineers of healthcare might fiercely and blindly promote digital technologies and virtual care models, this path has its own flaws.

Innovating the delivery of healthcare services and interventions via smartphones and connected devices is not the same as delivering movies into the home like Netflix. Innovating in healthcare can have life-and-death consequences for patients. At the same time, the current system is inadequate—and it also has life-and-death consequences for patients. In fact, in many cases, the biggest critics of new technology-driven models of care have been lulled into the belief that the current standards of care are the best we can do.[2] We, as those seeking to improve health among the population and for those patients who seek help, must not fall into the trap of becoming a pure Druid or Engineer. Instead, we must adopt the best characteristics of each.

From the Druids, we must bring skepticism, reasonable worry, and a fierce protection of our values and protection of human quality of life. As Druids, we must require the evidence and adopt a learning mindset. From the Engineers we must express a drive to solve problems for the sake of improvement, we must reject complacency, we must leverage science and technology, and we must be open to change. Engineers bring curiosity and a passion for building a better future.

The rapid development of digital technologies for healthcare will lead to plenty of snake oil. But, there will also be numerous innovations worth their salt—importantly, these early innovations will lead to knowledge that is replicable and scalable. The challenge going forward will be to ensure that we implement those that improve health outcomes, that are cost-efficient, and that improve patient and provider satisfaction.

The evidence for effective virtual care models has rapidly evolved since the early days of telemedicine as wearables and smartphones have led to new capabilities. From a wide field of digitally enhanced clinical models, technologies, and companies, we are beginning to see trends emerge. Certain program characteristics and combinations of interventions are showing promise. The positive clinical evidence speaks for itself.

These programs, when built properly, operationalize high-quality, high-touch models of care. For years, these types of approaches have been shot down by CFOs due to their high-cost, low-margin nature for healthcare organizations. But, the adoption of digital technologies solves these problems by automating manual processes and providing a new medium through which to engage with patients both passively and actively.

The preeminent model that is showing the most promise is one where mobile applications for RPM are used in conjunction with health coaching models staffed by a multilevel care team. In these models, it's not just about a 21.6-minute patient visit resulting in a prescription and an off-hand comment about diet and exercise; rather it is a continuous relationship along a health journey between care teams and patients. Virtual care, given the powerful data collection and improved communication, allows healthcare services to branch deeper through intervention into the multitude of factors that impact health.

*

For many, virtual care means little more than the use of technology to improve access to healthcare services on demand and for those without access to care at a physical location. As with traditional telemedicine, it is important to note that improved access to care for those without it is an impactful innovation in and of itself, but this is not all that virtual care can and should be.

For others, it is simply a market differentiator or competitive advantage. Consumers and patients want a Netflix-like experience, so organizations will simply adopt and cloak existing models of care under the guise of convenience and digital experiences.

But virtual care has the potential to bring so much more to healthcare services. Truly, the implementation of digital technologies into chronic care models has the potential to drive significantly improved patient engagement that leads to better health outcomes, improved patient experiences, and lower cost. Driven by both FFS reimbursement and value-based payment models, the convergence of payment innovation with virtual care will be a powerful force shaping healthcare's future.

Through your curiosity, I hope you will join us in the pursuit of better chronic care for our friends, family, and people around the world.

NOTES

1. John Brockman, et al. *What Should We Be Worried About? Real Scenarios That Keep Scientists Up at Night*. New York: Harper Perennial, 2014.

2. The drive for clinical evidence can lull some into the belief that there is an end state to clinical models. While a positive outcome evaluation of a program is positive, there is always room for improvement and continued experimentation. Real-time care models built on RPM allow for this kind of rapid evaluation and continuous improvement.

Index

Note: Page numbers in italics indicate a figure and page numbers in bold indicate a table on the corresponding page.

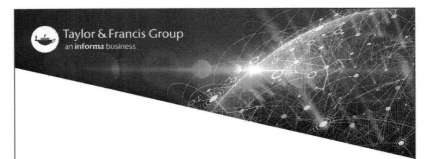